New+
GET UP TO SPEED

Situational

New Get Up to Speed + *Situational*
helps students learn how to speak like a native speaker
by focusing on contemporary language usage in everyday
situations supplemented with modern facts and cultural
notions.

Key Features
- Warm Up Activity
- Useful Phrases
- Slang & Idioms
- Key Conversation
- Situational Collocations
- What Would You Do?
- Cultural Discussion Questions
- If You Ask Me

MP3

CARROT HOUSE

6

CARROT HOUSE

New Get Up To Speed+ 6 Situational
© Carrot House

All rights reserved. No part of this publication may be reproduced,
stores in a retrieval system, or transmitted in any form or by any means
without the prior permission in writing of Carrot House.

Printed : First published January 2019
　　　　　Reprinted September 2019

Author : Carrot Language Lab

ISBN 978-89-6732-296-0

Printed and distributed in Korea
9F, 488, Gangnam St. Gangnam-gu, Seoul, 06120, South Korea

Curriculum Map

Course	Level 1	Level 2	Level 3	Level 4	Level 5	Level 6	Level 7	Text Book
General Conversation	Essential English : Begin Again							
	Pre Get Up to Speed 1~2							
		New Get Up to Speed+ 1~2						
			New Get Up to Speed+ 3~4					
				New Get Up to Speed+ 5~6				
					New Get Up to Speed+ 7~8			
	Daily Focused English 1							
		Daily Focused English 2						
Discussion				Active Discussion 1				
					Active Discussion 2			
						Dynamic Discussion		
				Chicken Soup Course				
				Dynamic Information & Digital Technology				
Business Conversation	Pre Business Basics 1							
		Pre Business Basics 2						
			Business Basics 1					
				Business Basics 2				
					Business Practice 1			
						Business Practice 2		
Global Biz Workshop				Effective Business Writing Skills (Workbook)				
				Effective Presentation Skills (Workbook)				
					Effective Negotiation Skills (Workbook)			
					Cross-Cultural Training 1~2 (Workbook)			
					Leadership Training Course (Workbook)			
Business Skills				Simple & Clear Technical Writing Skills				
				Effective Business Writing Skills				
				Effective Meeting Skills				
				Business Communication (Negotiation)				
				Effective Presentation Skills				
					Marketing 1			
						Marketing 2		
						Management		
On the Job English				Human Resources				
				Accounting and Finance				
				Marketing and Sales				
				Production Management				
				Automotive				
				Banking and Commerce				
				Medical and Medicine				
				Information Technology				
				Construction				
			Construction English in Use 1 ~ 4					
			Public Service English in Use					

※ This Curriculum Map illustrates the entire line-up of textbooks at CARROT HOUSE.

CARROT HOUSE _ 2019.01

"New⁺ GET UP TO SPEED
Situational

Introduction

Carrot House Methodology

Andragogical Approach & Productive English
The teaching of children (pedagogy) and adult learning (andragogy) are distinctively different. Pedagogy is akin to training and encourages convergent thinking and rote learning. It is compulsory, centered on the teacher and the imparting of information with minimal control by the learner. Andragogy, by contrast, is about education as freedom. It encourages divergent thinking and active learning. It is voluntary, learner oriented and opens up vistas for continual learning. Adults need to feel independent and in control of their learning. Therefore, Carrot House curriculum is based on andragogy and is designed to encourage learners' participation and engagement by providing more task-based activities and opportunities to frequently interact in the classroom. People want to achieve communicative competence when they learn other languages. English education in EFL environments has been rather focused on the receptive skills of English—listening and reading—which simply increases learners' knowledge about a language, not the competence of using it. If people are well equipped with productive skills—speaking and writing—they will be competent in English communication. This is why Carrot House curriculum is designed to enhance learners' productive skills throughout the course. This andragogical approach of the Carrot House Curriculum, which focuses on productive English, will enable learners to achieve communication skills necessary for global competence. Carrot House's teaching philosophy and curriculum combine to provide a "Language for Success" for all learners.

Communicative Language Learning (CLL)
This communicative interaction, the essential component of language acquisition, does not occur in a typical, non-meaningful, fun-oriented conversation with native speakers. It occurs in a negotiated interaction through which a well-trained teacher provides the comprehensible input that is appropriate to the learners. The learners, at the same time, actively utilize the opportunities given to them by the teachers. To this end, the Communicative Language Learning (CLL) method is employed in the field of Foreign Language Acquisition. The CLL method provides activities that are geared toward using language pragmatically, authentically and functionally with the intention of achieving meaningful purposes.

Course Overview

Features

Productive English
Learn to use practical and authentic expressions in various daily conversation, common collocations, written sentences, and activities.

Maximization of Schema
The use of visual texts, topic specific questions and useful expressions allow learners to find connections between the contents and their lives by maximizing their schema.

Interactive Activity
Activities, such as role-play, pair-work, group-work, and class-work, provide learners with the opportunity to constantly interact each other.

A Range of Everyday Topics
Through dealing with a range of daily situations in class, learners are equipped to tackle similar situations in reality.

Discussion
Learners can expand their ability to effectively express themselves in English through discussing a broad range of topics.

Slang / Idiom
Through learning topic-related slang and idioms, learners can improve their English language proficiency and use contemporary informal expressions to articulate their ideas.

Opinions on Topic-related Situations
Aims to enhance learner's abilities to speak logically. This task gives learners the chance to express their opinions on a given topic or from a choice of two situations.

Lesson Composition

Each New Get Up To Speed+ Situational book 5-8 is composed of 11 lessons.
Each lesson is composed of 8 main activities and 3 useful extra activities.

1. Warm Up Activity

To activate the students and their background knowledge, the lesson starts with discussing an image together with three situation-related-questions.

2. Useful Phrases

Students can improve and polish their English-language ability by practicing to integrate actively used phrases into their daily language.

3. Slang & Idioms

Reinforce the learner's ability to speak English like a native through the use of situational contemporary slang & idioms.

4. Key Conversation

Students can read, listen, and repeat how native speakers communicate with others on a daily basis. The activity also includes questions to test comprehension skills.

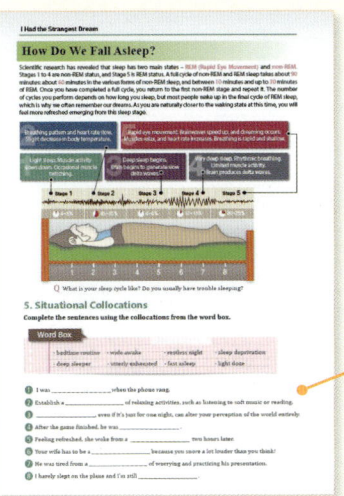

5. Situational Collocations

Students can improve and polish their English-language ability by learning and practicing how native speakers commonly group everyday words.

Lesson Composition

Each New Get Up To Speed+ Situational book 5-8 is composed of 11 lessons.
Each lesson is composed of 8 main activities and 3 useful extra activities.

6. What Would You Do?

Students can improve their comprehension and English word analyzing and discussion skills through geared situations and questions. This helps students practice their language-use for a wide variety of situations.

7. Cultural Discussion Questions

Gives the learners the opportunity to share, learn, and discuss global, cultural, and personal opinions and notions.

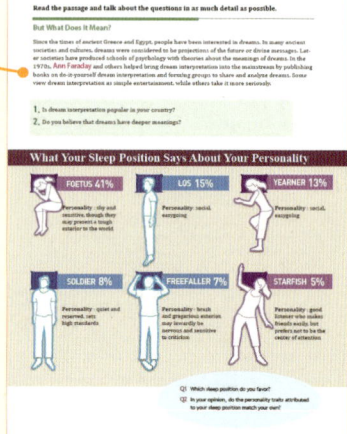

8. If You Ask Me

Gives the learners the opportunity to make a choice and share and defend their personal opinions of debatable issues.

Extra Activities

Each lesson includes three extra activities composed of engaging facts and figures. These activities provide students with both popular and intriguing global facts. These can also be used to help facilitate a more fun and enjoyable class.

Contents

Title	Learning Objective	Expression Check	
Lesson 1 I Had the Strangest Dream	To discuss sleep patterns and dreams.	- My sleep patterns are really out of whack these days. - I had this really vivid dream last night. - I've been burning the candle at both ends lately, and my sleep has really suffered.	10
Lesson 2 We're a Close Knit Bunch	To discuss creating bonds or friendships within a neighborhood.	- We've become quite close over the years. - Our neighbors are like extensions of our family. - News travels quickly through a tightly knit community.	16
Lesson 3 Eastern vs. Western	To discuss cultural differences between Eastern and Western countries.	- Does your society really benefit from a six-day workweek? - Parents in Western countries don't feel the need for after-school academic programs. - Eastern and Western societies have different ideas about raising children.	22
Lesson 4 If I Could Change One Thing	To express regret about past actions.	- I wish I didn't' travel as much when you kids were young. - I feel like I was never there when you kids were growing up. - I should've done a better job of prioritizing work and family.	28
Lesson 5 International Relations	To discuss relationships between countries.	- Free trade agreements can be mutually beneficial for all countries involved. - It's in the best interest of each country to strike an accord. - The problem with governments these days is that they're just in it for themselves.	34
Lesson 6 Prepping for an Emergency	To discuss natural disasters and how to prepare for them.	- In the event of a… - Whatever you do, don't… - The first thing you should do during a…	40
Lesson 7 Our Top Story Tonight	To discuss headline news and current events.	- Did you happen to catch the evening news and hear about…? - It's hard to believe something so tragic could actually happen. - This story will certainly spark a lot of debate.	46
Lesson 8 Moving On From a Setback	To handle and react to personal and professional setbacks.	- I'm turning the page—this is a new chapter in my life. - On to bigger and better things. - I'm just taking life one day at a time.	52
Lesson 9 I Downloaded It Last Night	To share your opinion on media sharing and downloads.	- I found this great website for downloading music and movies. - The problem with this is the artist is cut out of any royalties. - I have no qualms about downloading movies off the internet.	58
Lesson 10 Travel Delays	To handle missing a scheduled flight.	- I missed my flight. Do you have another one available before 3:00? - I'm sorry, but the flight has been overbooked. I can offer you a seat on the next one. - Is it possible for my baggage to be checked through to my final destination?	64
Lesson 11 International Conflict	To discuss international diplomacy.	- These two countries have been at odds for as long as I can remember. - This is a perfect example of what conflict can do. - One of these countries needs to extend the olive branch.	70
Lesson 12 I Wish I'd Done Something Differently	To express regret for things you have or haven't done.	- I'm never doing that again as long as I live. - I totally regret taking my parents' advice. - I wish I would've just followed my heart.	76

Slang & Idioms	82
Answer Key	84

01 I Had the Strangest Dream

Learning Objective
Upon completion of this lesson you will be able to **discuss sleep patterns and dreams.**

Expression Check

- ☑ My sleep patterns are really out of whack these days.
- ☑ I had this really vivid dream last night.
- ☑ I've been burning the candle at both ends lately, and my sleep has really suffered.

1. Warm Up Activity

Talk about the questions.

1. Do you usually remember your dreams?
2. Have you ever had a dream that played out in real life?
3. Have you ever had a recurring dream or a very bad nightmare?

2. Useful Phrases

Match the phrases (a-d) to the phrases (1-4) to form a complete sentence. The useful phrases are italicized.

A We usually *sleep in*

B Ever since he lost his job,

C Once things get settled,

D *I didn't get a wink of sleep* last night

1 on the weekend.

2 with all that noise outside.

3 I'm sure *you'll be sleeping soundly again.*

4 *he's been tossing and turning* all night.

3. Slang & Idioms

Check out the slang and idioms and try to make your own sentences.

A **snooze** : to sleep for a short period — *I'm just going to snooze for a few minutes before the movie.*

B **shuteye** : sleep — *You look like you're in need of some shuteye.*

C **catch some Z's** : to get some sleep — *I'm heading home to catch some Z's.*

D **catnap** : a short, light sleep; a doze — *You'll feel better if you take a catnap before dinner.*

4. Key Conversation

Read through the dialogue and practice with a partner.

Too Tired to Sleep

Bill	I feel absolutely horrible! I didn't get a wink of sleep last night.
George	Really? Why not? I thought that project you were so worried about was finished. Why didn't you sleep?
Bill	Well, the project is finished, but I had been burning the candle at both ends for so long that my sleep has really suffered. I guess I'm actually too tired to sleep!
George	Goodness! You have to get some shuteye sometime, or you'll get sick!
Bill	I know, but my sleep patterns are really out of whack these days. I manage to fall asleep, but before I can get into a really deep sleep, I wake up and can't get back to sleep again.
George	Wow! That sounds like a really bad case of insomnia. Be careful. Have you tried a glass of warm milk?
Bill	I hate warm milk, and besides, that's an old wives' tale–it doesn't work.
George	Maybe you should see a doctor.
Bill	I guess so. I'll see about going today after work.
George	Sweet dreams!

Questions

1. Which man do you think has been working harder lately?
2. Do you think George's advice was helpful?

I Had the Strangest Dream

How Do We Fall Asleep?

Scientific research has revealed that sleep has two main states – **REM (Rapid Eye Movement)** and **non-REM**. Stages 1 to 4 are non-REM status, and Stage 5 is REM status. A full cycle of non-REM and REM sleep takes about **90** minutes: about **60** minutes in the various forms of non-REM sleep, and between **10** minutes and up to **30** minutes of REM. Once you have completed a full cycle, you return to the first non-REM stage and repeat it. The number of cycles you perform depends on how long you sleep, but most people wake up in the final cycle of REM sleep, which is why we often remember our dreams. As you are naturally closer to the waking state at this time, you will feel more refreshed emerging from this sleep stage.

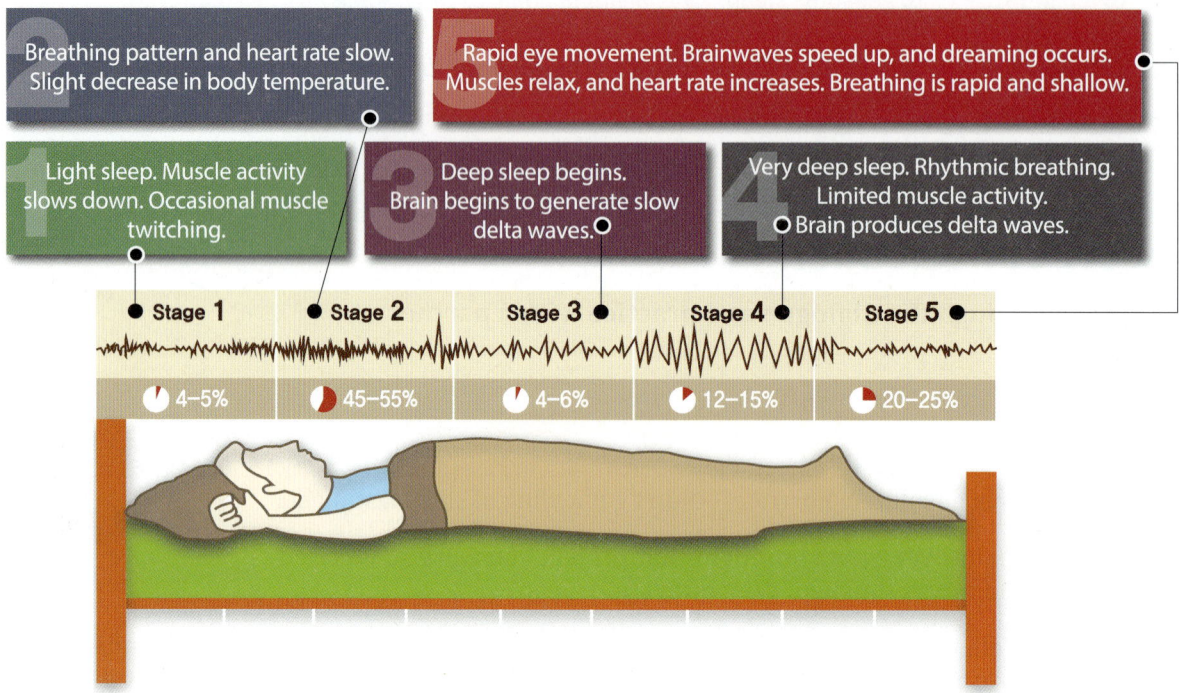

Q What is your sleep cycle like? Do you usually have trouble sleeping?

5. Situational Collocations

Complete the sentences using the collocations from the word box.

Word Box

| · bedtime routine | · wide awake | · restless night | · sleep deprivation |
| · deep sleeper | · utterly exhausted | · fast asleep | · light doze |

❶ I was _____ when the phone rang.

❷ Establish a _____ of relaxing activities, such as listening to soft music or reading.

❸ _____, even if it's just for one night, can alter your perception of the world entirely.

❹ After the game finished, he was _____ .

❺ Feeling refreshed, she woke from a _____ two hours later.

❻ Your wife has to be a _____ because you snore a lot louder than you think!

❼ He was tired from a _____ of worrying and practicing his presentation.

❽ I barely slept on the plane and I'm still _____ .

6. What Would You Do?

Read the situation and explain what you would do in that situation.

You Need to See a Sleep Specialist

You have been having the same dream off and on over the past few weeks. As time goes by, the dream turns into a nightmare and involves people in your circle of friends and family. You begin to abhor the thought of going to bed and having the dream. The dream is becoming more and more vivid; as a result, you are getting less and less sleep. Your friends and co-workers have started to notice that you do not look well. You confide in your mother and best friend and tell them about the dream. Your best friend suggests consulting a sleep specialist, and your mother suggests getting your dream analyzed.

Q1. How would you handle your problem?
Q2. What do you think could be causing your bad dreams?
Q3. How do you feel after having a bad dream?

How Did You *Sleep Last Night?*

Many people have trouble fitting their busy lives into a 24-hour day and see nothing wrong with sleeping less than 6 hours a night. While doing this occasionally is nothing to worry about, a good night's sleep is a basic necessity for a healthy life. Not only does sleep give us the necessary energy to carry out our daily tasks, long-term sleep deprivation can also have serious consequences for your health.

1 How much sleep do we need?

NEWBORNS 0-2 months	12 - 18 HOURS	
INFANTS 3 months to 1 years	14 - 15 HOURS	
TODDLERS 1 to 3 years	12 - 14 HOURS	
PRESCHOOLERS 3 to 5 years	11 - 12 HOURS	
SCHOOL-AGED CHILDREN 5 to 12 years	10 - 11 HOURS	
TEENS AND PRETEENS 12 to 15 years	8.5 - 10 HOURS	
ADULTS 15+	7.5 - 9 HOURS	

2 Why is sleep deprivation dangerous?

RISK OF CANCER
The likelihood of breast cancer is doubled for those who go to sleep too late
LESS SLEEP » + 200% RISK

RISK OF HEART DISEASE
The risk of a heart attack increases by 100% for those who sleep for less than 7hrs per night
LESS SLEEP » + 100% RISK

OBESITY
Instead watching TV, try to sleep 1hr more and see how you lose 6.5 kg per year
MORE SLEEP » - 6.5 KG PER YEAR

RISK OF DEATH
Not getting enough sleep means that you are 20% more likely to die in 20 years
LESS SLEEP » + 20% RISK

Q1 How many hours do you sleep on an average day?
Q2 In order to be at your best, how many hours of sleep do you think you need?

I Had the Strangest Dream

7. Cultural Discussion Questions

Read the passage and talk about the questions in as much detail as possible.

But What Does It Mean?

Since the times of ancient Greece and Egypt, people have been interested in dreams. In many ancient societies and cultures, dreams were considered to be projections of the future or divine messages. Later societies have produced schools of psychology with theories about the meanings of dreams. In the 1970s, Ann Faraday and others helped bring dream interpretation into the mainstream by publishing books on do-it-yourself dream interpretation and forming groups to share and analyze dreams. Some view dream interpretation as simple entertainment, while others take it more seriously.

1. Is dream interpretation popular in your country?
2. Do you believe that dreams have deeper meanings?

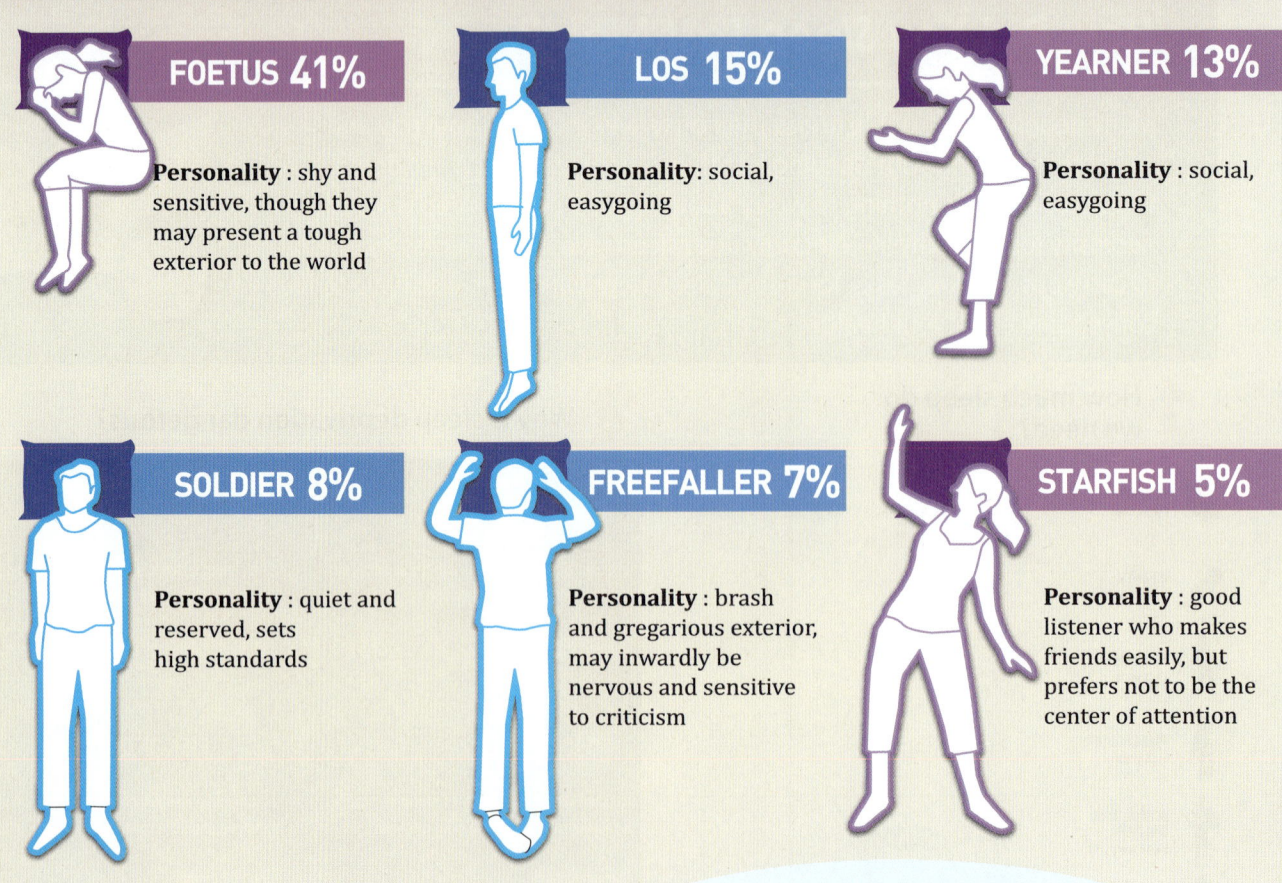

What Your Sleep Position Says About Your Personality

- **FOETUS 41%** — **Personality**: shy and sensitive, though they may present a tough exterior to the world
- **LOS 15%** — **Personality**: social, easygoing
- **YEARNER 13%** — **Personality**: social, easygoing
- **SOLDIER 8%** — **Personality**: quiet and reserved, sets high standards
- **FREEFALLER 7%** — **Personality**: brash and gregarious exterior, may inwardly be nervous and sensitive to criticism
- **STARFISH 5%** — **Personality**: good listener who makes friends easily, but prefers not to be the center of attention

Q1 Which sleep position do you favor?
Q2 In your opinion, do the personality traits attributed to your sleep position match your own?

Lesson 01 / I Had the Strangest Dream   15

8. If You Ask Me

Read the discussion topic and select the statement that you believe in the most. Then role-play the scenario.

Do You Remember Your Dreams?

Some people are adamant that they do not dream. However, scientific researchers disagree. Scientists who have studied the different stages of sleep and sleep patterns assure us that, whether we choose to believe it or not, everyone dreams. Our dreams occur during the REM (Rapid Eye Movement) stages of sleep, which everyone goes through.

Topic Question

People who claim they never dream do so because they simply do not remember their dreams.

Do you think that everyone dreams or only some people do?

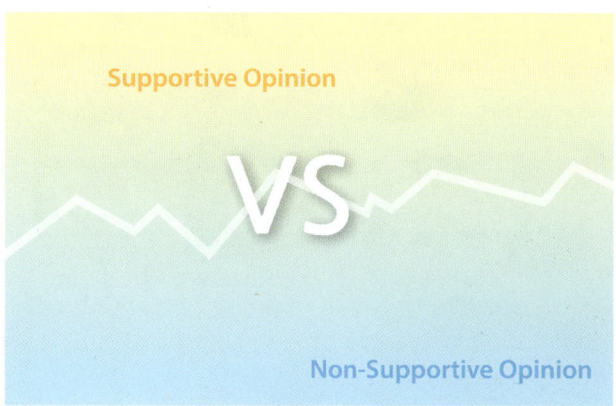

Supportive Opinion

VS

Non-Supportive Opinion

Role-play

Act out the role-play using the slang and idioms and useful expressions.

Situation

You are telling your friend about a terrifying dream that you had last night. In your dream, you were kidnapped and desperately wanted to escape. When you had a chance to run, you found yourself paralyzed with fear and you were unable to move. Even after you woke up, you felt scared and hopeless. You are curious about what you think the dream means and want to get your friend's opinion.

Role A
- Describe your dream to your friend.
- Ask his or her opinion.

Role B
- Ask your friend if he or she has been experiencing a lot of stress lately.
- Assure your friend that the dream is normal.

Wrapping Up!   Tell four things that you learned from this lesson and review.

1	2	3	4

02 We're a Close Knit Bunch

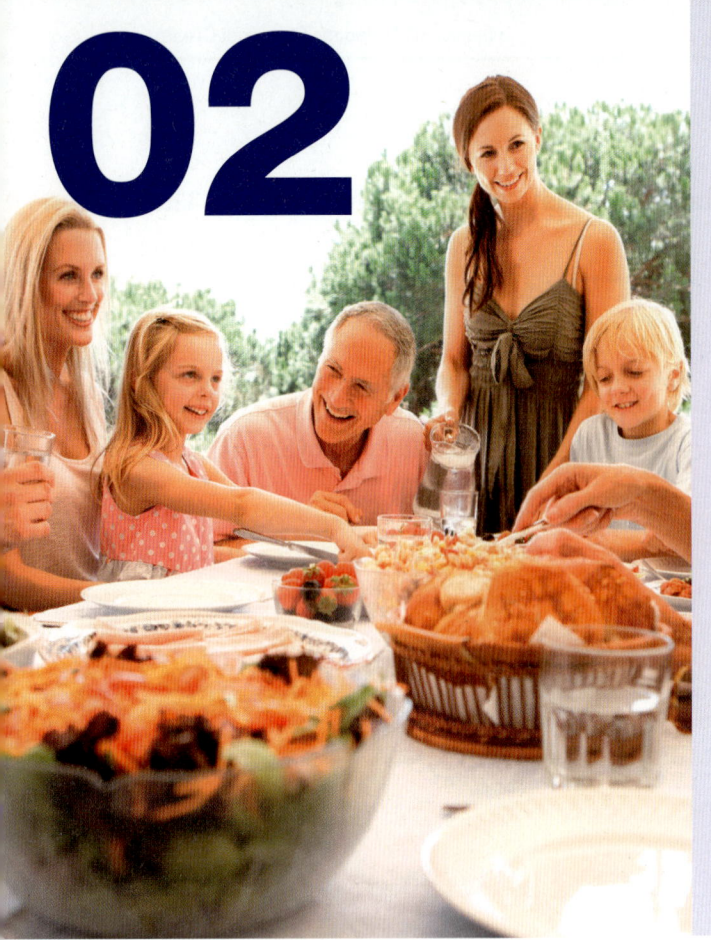

Learning Objective
Upon completion of this lesson you will be able to **discuss creating bonds or friendships within a neighborhood.**

Expression Check
- ☑ We've become quite close over the years.
- ☑ Our neighbors are like extensions of our family.
- ☑ News travels quickly through a tightly knit community.

1. Warm Up Activity
Talk about the questions.

1. Do you know your current neighbors? If so, do you socialize with them?
2. How important do you think it is to be friendly with your neighbors? Explain.
3. Have you ever had a really close friend who was also a neighbor?

2. Useful Phrases
Match the phrases (a-d) to the phrases (1-4) to form a complete sentence. The useful phrases are italicized.

A Since we first met in college,

B I work with some great people.

C I shoveled the snow on his sidewalk.

D This is my friend Tom.

1 We're *like one, big happy family.*

2 He and I *go back for years.*

3 we've *grown quite close over the years.*

4 *It was the neighborly thing to do.*

3. Slang & Idioms

Check out the slang and idioms and try to make your own sentences.

A	**block party** : a party for all the residents of a block or neighborhood	Are you planning on stopping by the block party later?
B	**fair-weather friend** : a person who stops being a friend in times of difficulty	I thought Gene would always stick by me, but he turned out to be a fair-weather friend.
C	**next-door neighbor** : a person living in the house or apartment closest to one's own	She's been my next-door neighbor for nearly 10 years.
D	**tightly-knit** : united or bound together by strong relationships and common interests	The tightly-knit mining communities had their own traditions and tales.

4. Key Conversation

🎧 Read through the dialogue and practice with a partner.

We're Like One, Big, Happy Family!

Gwen	Hey, Suzanne! Are you all settled in? How's your new apartment?
Suzanne	It's great! Thank you so much for helping me find it. I can't believe we're actually going to be neighbors in the same building! First, roommates at school, now neighbors!
Gwen	You'll love living here. Wait till you meet the others in the building.
Suzanne	You mean you know the other people who have apartments in this building? You actually know your neighbors?
Gwen	Yes! And you'll too, very soon! There's going to be a roof party this weekend. You'll see. We've become quite close over the years. We're like one, big, happy family!
Suzanne	Really! How interesting, a roof party!
Gwen	That's nothing! Wait till the block party next month!
Suzanne	You're kidding! A block party! Now I know why you insisted I move into the neighborhood.

Questions

1. Do you think Suzanne will like her neighbors in the new building?
2. In your opinion, have Suzanne and Gwen been friends for a long time?

We're a Close Knit Bunch

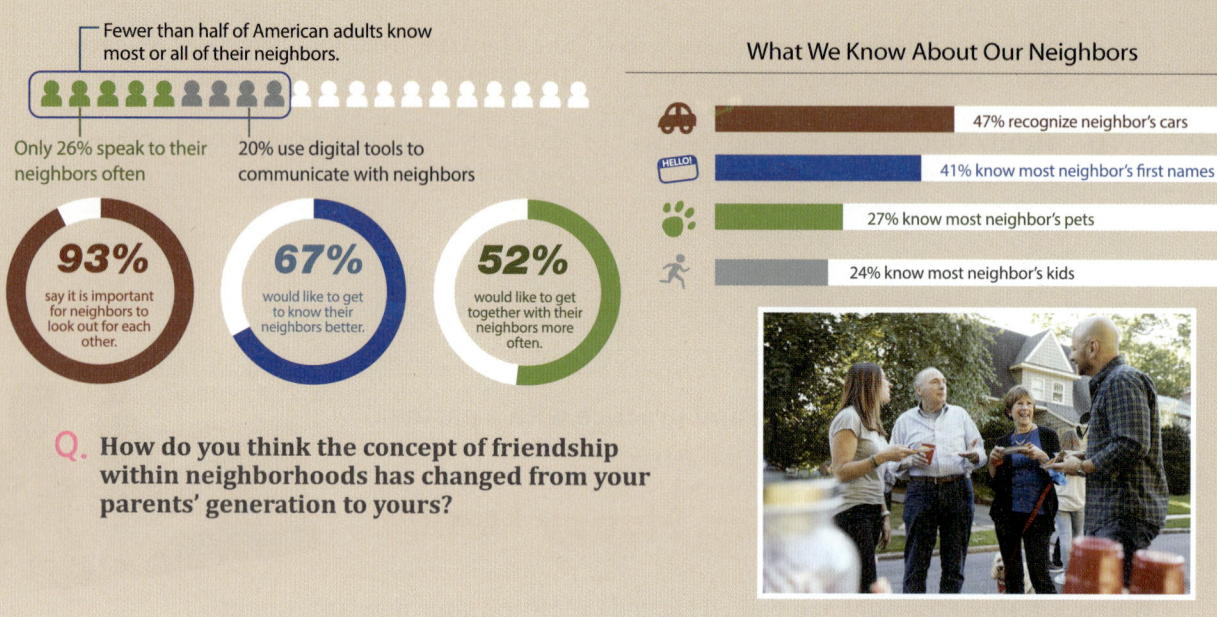

Neighborly Relations

How close are you to your neighbors? A recent survey revealed that fewer than half of Americans know theirs well, but 93% still believe that neighbors should look out for one another and 52% would like to get together with their neighbors more often.

- Fewer than half of American adults know most or all of their neighbors.
- Only 26% speak to their neighbors often
- 20% use digital tools to communicate with neighbors

93% say it is important for neighbors to look out for each other

67% would like to get to know their neighbors better.

52% would like to get together with their neighbors more often.

What We Know About Our Neighbors
- 47% recognize neighbor's cars
- 41% know most neighbor's first names
- 27% know most neighbor's pets
- 24% know most neighbor's kids

Q. How do you think the concept of friendship within neighborhoods has changed from your parents' generation to yours?

5. Situational Collocations

Complete the sentences using the collocations from the word box.

Word Box

- closely related
- considerable hospitality
- lifelong friendship
- warm smile
- get together
- drop by
- friendly approach
- welcoming committee

1. Hannah and Jessica get along because they are _____.
2. His _____ to business sets him apart from most people in the industry.
3. My aunt welcomed us into her home with a _____ and a hug.
4. The _____ stopped by with a few things to introduce us to the neighborhood.
5. We were astounded by the _____ they showed us during our stay.
6. The two men became close and developed a _____.
7. I just want to _____ with friends and watch a movie or something.
8. We thought we would _____ and welcome you to the neighborhood.

6. What Would You Do?

Read the situation and explain what you would do in that situation.

You have been living in your current apartment for the last five years and have made very good friendships with the other people in the building as well as in the neighborhood. At the request of your family, one of your cousins has come to live with you until he finds a job and gets his own place. Although you have explained to your cousin about the relationships that you have with others in the building and neighborhood, he does not seem to care. Your cousin is cold, unfriendly and occasionally rude to your neighbors. His behavior has been so off-putting that you even received an official notice from the apartment management company requesting that your cousin leave the apartment.

Q1. What would you say to your cousin?

Q2. In this case, what would be more important to you: neighbors or family?

Q3. How could you make it up to your neighbors?

Good Neighbor Day

+53%

Are you a good neighbor? Or do you have good neighbors? The concept of National Good Neighbor Day began in the early 1970s when Montana resident Becky Mattson pushed to create a holiday that would recognize people who make their neighborhoods a great place to live.

The annual event became a National Holiday in 2003 when US Senator Max Baucus sponsored a US resolution naming **Sept. 28 National Good Neighbor Day.** It is important to just be the best neighbor you can be and thank the good ones for being a part of your life.

One of the studies about neighbors says that knowing your neighbor could save your life. In reality, the chances of surviving a stroke improved by **53%** for seniors living in friendly neighborhood environments.

Q. Does your neighborhood host any events to encourage friendship between residents? If not, would you like to attend such an event?

7. Cultural Discussion Questions

Read the passage and talk about the questions in as much detail as possible.

Are You a Good Neighbor

In many Western countries, it is common for people to take the time to establish good relationships with their neighbors. In addition to social benefits, being friendly with one's neighbors makes the community a safer and more comfortable place to live. Neighbors watch out for one another and even may offer to help take care of others' pets and property while they are away. When moving into a neighborhood, it is important to introduce yourself to your neighbors and to touch base regularly with your neighbors to make sure that everything is going well in your community.

1. Is it common to maintain close relationships with neighbors in your country?
2. How can you make friends when moving to a new neighborhood?

What Your Communication Style Says About Your Relationships With Neighbors

Americans use a range of approaches to keep informed about what is happening in their communities. The graph shows the findings from a survey conducted among **2,258 Americans.** Interestingly, the tools people use to keep up with community issues are related to whether or not they are on a first-name basis with their neighbors. As people know fewer of their neighbors by name, they become much less likely to discuss community issues face-to-face.

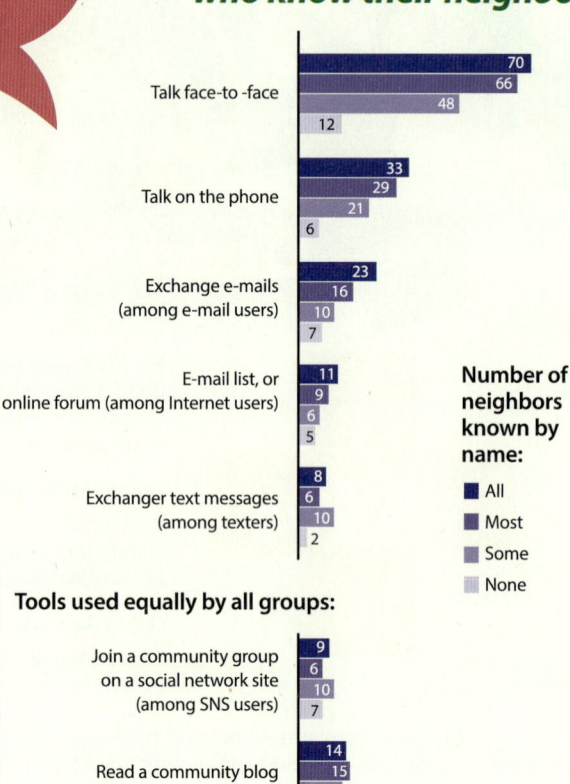

Q1. Are you the kind of person who likes to get to know your neighbors?

Q2. How do you prefer to communicate with your neighbors? Why?

Lesson 02 / We're a Close Knit Bunch 21

8. If You Ask Me

Read the discussion topic and select the statement that you believe in the most. Then role-play the scenario.

Should I Stay or Should I Go?

You just moved into a new apartment in an unfamiliar neighborhood. You are a very private person, but since the first day you moved in, your neighbors have been knocking on your door nonstop. Everyone wants to introduce themselves or offer to show you around the neighborhood. They all seem very sincere and friendly, but you are not used to having so much contact with your neighbors and the attention is making you uncomfortable. A few people even mentioned that they are hosting a "Getting to Know You" party in your honor in two weeks.

Topic Question

Would you graciously accept the kindness of your new neighbors and try to fit in? Or would you politely refuse their invitations and continue to keep to yourself?

Supportive Opinion **VS** Non-Supportive Opinion

Role-play

Act out the role-play using the slang and idioms and useful expressions.

Situation
A new tenant recently moved next door to you. One day, you are baking a cake and discover that you don't have enough sugar, so you go next door and borrow some from your neighbor. After you finish baking, you decide that you should go next door and offer a piece to your neighbor as a token of gratitude. Your neighbor seems nice and you would like to become friends.

Role A
- Thank your neighbor again for the sugar.
- Ask how he or she likes the new neighborhood.

Role B
- Thank your neighbor for coming by.
- Invite your neighbor in to talk.

Wrapping Up!

Tell four things that you learned from this lesson and review.

1	2	3	4

03 Eastern vs. Western

Learning Objective

Upon completion of this lesson you will be able to **discuss cultural differences between Eastern and Western countries.**

Expression Check

- ☑ Does your society really benefit from a five-day workweek?
- ☑ Parents in Western countries don't feel the need for after-school academic programs.
- ☑ Eastern and Western societies have different ideas about raising children.

1. Warm Up Activity

Talk about the questions.

1. What do you feel is your culture's greatest contribution to the world?
2. When people think about your culture, what do they usually think of?
3. What surprises you the most when you interact with people from different cultures?

2. Useful Phrases

Match the phrases (a-d) to the phrases (1-4) to form a complete sentence. The useful phrases are italicized.

A Does your society *really benefit from*

B Parents in Western countries *don't feel the need for*

C Eastern and Western societies

D Individualism *is a quality valued in*

1 after-school academic programs.

2 *have different ideas about* raising children.

3 a five-day workweek?

4 Western culture.

3. Slang & Idioms

Check out the slang and idioms and try to make your own sentences.

A	**closed-minded** : unreceptive to new ideas or arguments	It's hard to argue with, much less convince, a closed-minded person.
B	**sheltered** : protected from difficulties or unpleasant realities	She led a sheltered life where she was unaware of the difficulties of those less fortunate.
C	**set aside one's differences** : to forget about or set aside the things that one disagrees with	Let's try to set aside our differences and see things from another perspective.
D	**as different as night and day** : as different as possible	Although we are brothers, we are as different as night and day.

4. Key Conversation

Read through the dialogue and practice with a partner.

Negi's Mother

Narita	Thank you for meeting with me on such short notice, teacher.
Jane	Please, call me Jane. We don't need to use formalities here. You're Negi's mother, right?
Narita	Yes, I just thought that I would check how you are enjoying your new job. You've only been teaching Negi's class for a month, right?
Jane	Things are great, but I don't think I'll ever get used to having to work six days a week.
Narita	Of course, but the kids need the extra time to study for their exams. It is very important because those scores can get them into a good university and later a good job. Parents here care a lot about their children's success.
Jane	I guess that makes sense. In America, we don't worry much about putting our children in after-school academies. We just want them to enjoy being kids.
Narita	But don't you worry if they will be able to get good jobs later?
Jane	Of course we are about their futures, but we also think they should have the freedom to make their own choices, you know?
Narita	Yes. Negi keeps telling me about how much he enjoys your classes, but I rarely see him doing any homework, so I'm concerned about him. In fact, I was hoping that you could tell me how I could help him to become a better student.
Jane	That's what I thought you wanted to know. Here, I'll show you how he's been doing.

Questions

1. Why do you think Narita asked to meet Jane?
2. Do you prefer Narita's values about raising her children, or Jane's?

Eastern vs. Western

Differing Perception

According to researchers from the University of Michigan, Asians and Westerners really do see the world differently. When looking at an image, people of European descent tend to pay more attention to the object in the foreground of a scene, while students from East Asia focus more on the background and the scene as a whole. Western culture emphasizes personal autonomy and formal logic, so Westerners are more analytic and pay attention to particular objects and categories. Being raised in a culture that emphasizes group harmony, East Asians view images and think in a more holistic way. They pay attention to all the elements of a scene and the relationships between items.

Q. What are some other differences between Eastern and Western culture that you know about?

5. Situational Collocations
Complete the sentences using the collocations from the word box.

Word Box

- fundamental differences
- social setting
- direct manner
- intercultural communication
- mainstream acceptance
- show respect
- starting point
- diverse viewpoints

❶ Wouldn't it be better for _____ if both local and foreign students were able to study in the international schools?

❷ Happily, today our society is more tolerant and open-minded and accepting of _____ .

❸ The idea gained _____ after the book hit the bestseller list.

❹ There are several _____ between the two cultures.

❺ It's very frustrating not being able to communicate well in a _____ .

❻ From the moment I met her, she won me over with her _____ and determination.

❼ The local culture emphasizes to _____ for elders.

❽ Assumptions are viewed as a _____ for reasoning.

6. What Would You Do?

Read the situation and explain what you would do in that situation.

You just moved to a new country for work and your son has enrolled in the local international school. The academic environment seems much more serious than his old school, so you signed him up for additional after-school classes to help him adapt to his new environment. Eager to succeed, your child often stays up late studying and finishing his homework. One day, you receive a letter from your child's teacher asking you to come into school to talk about a problem. The teacher is concerned that your son keeps falling asleep in class.

Q1. What would you say to your son's teacher?

Q2. Would you continue to encourage your son to study or would you ask him to relax?

Q3. What other challenges might a child face in a new school? How could you help your son cope?

Between the East and West

Read through the following list of cultural differences between Eastern and Western cultures.

East	West
Live in 'time'	Live in 'space'
Value rest and relaxation	Value activity
Passive, accepting	Assertive, confronting
Contemplative	Diligent
Accept what is	Seek change
Live in nature (part of nature itself)	Live with nature (co-existing with nature)
Want to know meaning	Want to know how it works
Freedom of silence	Freedom of speech
Lapse into meditation	Strive for articulation
Focus on consideration of others' feelings	Focus on self-assuredness, own needs
Learn to do with less material assets	Attempt to get more of everything
Honor austerity	Honor achievement
Retire to enjoy the gift of one's family	Retire to enjoy the rewards of one's work

Eastern-Western friendships can be extremely successful as long as both parties make an effort to understand and accept differences in each other's culture and traditions. It's natural to think 'our way' is best, but keeping an open mind is important when establishing a healthy relationship with someone else.

> Q. Have you ever had a conflict with someone else from a different cultural background? How did you try to resolve the conflict?

Eastern vs. Western

7. Cultural Discussion Questions

Read the passage and talk about the questions in as much detail as possible.

Cultural Values

Conflict and misunderstandings often occur between different cultures because of underlying values that the culture holds dear. Below are some examples of values held by Westerners from North America and their contrasting value.

	Cultural Value	Contrasting Value
PERSONAL SPACE	For many North Americans, personal space is very important. If someone comes too close, most will move away. On many subways, seats will often be left empty if the seat directly beside it has someone sitting there. Personal property is also considered very important.	Space Conservation: often spaces are very crowded, and standing close to one another is not seen as a very significant problem. In some cases, property is also shared between individuals if there is a need.
CONTROL OF THE FUTURE	People can alter the direction of their lives and of their environment. There is an entrepreneurial drive to better themselves and a desire to choose their own destiny.	Fatalism: You are born into your circumstances (rich vs. poor, country, culture, karma), and you cannot escape what has already been decided by factors before you were born.
DIRECT, HONEST	Honesty is seen as the best policy. It is better to state your mind and express yourself openly, whether with new ideas, plans, proposals, or criticisms. "Beating around the bush" is looked upon with impatience.	Saving Face: People should consider the feelings of the other person and their relationship before saying what they want to say. Often speech is indirect. Subtle hints and clues are better than blurting out your disfavor with the other person.
INFORMAL	First name usage ("Call me John"), casual clothes, a distrust of formal ritual and hierarchy. A person is treated the same whether older, younger, male or female. Trust and respect are earned based on performance.	Formal Hierarchy: Formal titles and family names are common, hierarchical relationships based on age, gender, marital status, and social rank. People are generally restrained and polite with one another.

Q1. Where does your country stand on these four cultural values?

Q2. What are some ways that your country's cultural values differ from others?

Western vs. Eastern Values

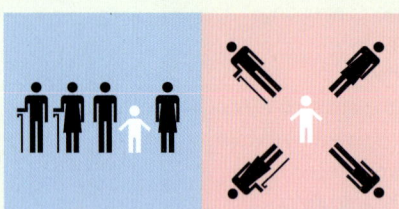

Parenting

In most Western countries, children are raised by their parents with limited help from other relatives. In Eastern countries, a child is looked after not only by the parents but also by both sets of grandparents.

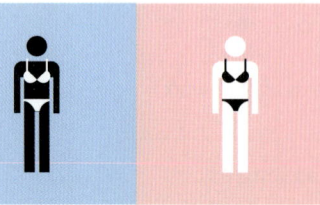

Perception of Beauty

In many Eastern countries, light skin is seen as ideal. People go to great extremes to avoid the sun. Asian women often use skin whitening beauty products and cover their skin while outdoors while Western women use self-tanning lotions and embrace the sun.

Q Have you ever worked with a Westerner? What cultural differences did you experience?

Lesson 03 / Eastern vs. Western **27**

8. If You Ask Me

Read the discussion topic and select the statement that you believe in the most. Then role-play the scenario.

Private Tutoring – GOOD OR BAD?

Private tutoring and after-school academies are extremely popular in some East Asian countries. Every day, tens of thousands of children attend classes to learn everything from foreign languages to art and sports. While institutes often promise parents that their children will score higher on tests and go on to live successful lives, many people have begun to question whether it is worth it. To pay for these extra classes, parents must sacrifice saving for their own retirement or even purchasing essential things for their household. In addition, long days of studying exhaust children and deprive them of time with their family and friends.

Topic Question

Do you think that after-school academies and private tutoring are worthwhile?

Supportive Opinion VS **Non-Supportive Opinion**

Role-play

Act out the role-play using the slang and idioms and useful expressions.

Situation

You have just returned to your home country after four years abroad at one of your company's overseas branches. Your boss would like to talk to you about the differences that you observed while living and working in a Western country. Tell him or her about what you enjoyed and what you found difficult.

Role A
- Tell your boss about some of the things you found different.
- Explain how the differences made you feel.

Role B
- Ask if there are any differences that could improve the working environment of your office.
- Thank your employee for expressing his or her opinion.

 **Tell four things that you learned from this lesson and review.**

| 1 | 2 | 3 | 4 |

04 If I Could Change One Thing

Learning Objective
Upon completion of this lesson you will be able to **express regret about past actions**.

Expression Check
- ☑ I wish I hadn't traveled as much when you kids were young.
- ☑ I feel like I was never there when you kids were growing up.
- ☑ I should've done a better job of prioritizing work and family.

1. Warm Up Activity
Talk about the questions.

1. If you could change one thing about your past, what would it be?
2. Do you sometimes wish you had taken a different path?
3. Have you ever missed any opportunities for unexpected reasons?

2. Useful Phrases
Match the phrases (a-d) to the phrases (1-4) to form a complete sentence. The useful phrases are italicized.

A. *I wish I didn't have to*

B. *I feel like I was*

C. *I should've done a better job*

D. *I'm sorry I was never*

1. prioritizing work and family.
2. never there while you kids were growing up.
3. there for you guys.
4. travel so much when you kids were young.

3. Slang & Idioms

Check out the slang and idioms and try to make your own sentences.

A	**latchkey kid** : a child who is at home without adult supervision for some part of the day	I was a latchkey kid, but I also helped out in my parents' store and made deliveries.
B	**kick oneself** : to blame or criticize oneself for something one has done	I'm kicking myself for not backing up the file.
C	**cry over spilled milk** : to express regret about something that has already happened or cannot be changed	Yes, we made a mistake, but there's no point in crying over spilled milk.
D	**live in the past** : to always be thinking about things that have already happened	There's no use in living in the past.

Don't Cry Over Spilt Milk

4. Key Conversation

 Read through the dialogue and practice with a partner.

Money vs. Memories

Jared	Hey Sam. Is everything all right?
Sam	Yeah, but my daughter's graduation is coming up this weekend, and the boss wants me back on the road again.
Jared	Oh man, that's tough! Can't you book this weekend off or find someone else to cover? I mean, your daughter only graduates from high school once.
Sam	I know. I've already missed so much of my kids' lives because I'm always working. I wasn't there for them while they were growing up.
Jared	Yes, but at least you were able to afford many of the things my family couldn't. I wish we had more money growing up, so I could provide all I can for my family.
Sam	A word of advice, Jared. Don't be so focused trying to make money that you miss the memories. I can't tell you how many times I kicked myself for missing Emily's dance recitals, or Tanya's plays, or Brian's soccer matches.
Jared	So, you regret all of the success you've had? I mean, branch manager of one of the biggest companies in the country is something to be proud of.
Sam	Jared, you'll learn one day that family is more important. I just wish someone would have told me that when I was your age.

Questions
1. Do you think Sam is happy about his success?
2. Do you think Sam is giving Jared good advice about how to prioritize his life?

If I Could Change One Thing

The Wheel of Life

The Wheel of Life is a tool used to conceptualize and identify areas of our lives that are out of balance. Areas that end closer to the center receive a lower level of personal investment in terms of time and effort, while those that end closer to the edge of the circle require a greater personal investment.

Look at the wheel on the left-hand side. You'll notice that this person seems to devote more energy to their business/career priorities than other areas and seemingly values money a lot. However, they are lacking in fun time and might be suffering in terms of health and personal growth opportunities.

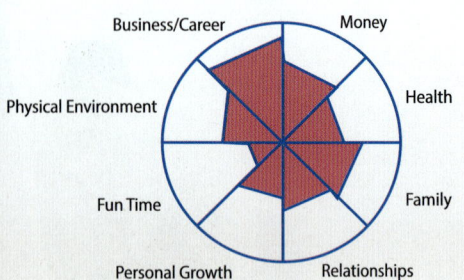
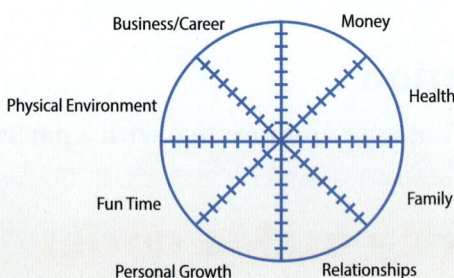

TASK: Consider your own priorities in life. Then, complete the wheel provided. After completing your wheel of life, consider how well it would run if it were an actual wheel. If you notice some imbalances in you wheel, do not worry. The objective of this wheel is to try to make strategic adjustments to reduce tension levels and achieve a smoother ride.

5. Situational Collocations

Complete the sentences using the collocations from the word box.

Word Box

- regrets bitterly
- work-life balance
- seized an opportunity
- juggling responsibilities
- opportunity cost
- deeply regretted
- take a day
- spending quality time

1. I've been looking forward to _____ with my children.
2. You should _____ to relax and do something you enjoy.
3. I've always _____ not being home more when my kids were young.
4. He _____ to go out of town with his family.
5. I'm currently struggling with the issue of _____.
6. It's difficult _____ like you do.
7. She _____ what she has done.
8. The _____ of doing something worthwhile with that money will be lost.

6. What Would You Do?

Read the situation and explain what you would do in that situation.

A Chance to Become a Star

While discussing regrets about the past, your best friend opens up about how he/she had the opportunity to act in a movie alongside a very well-known actor during his/her younger years. He/she tells you that he/she turned down the opportunity because he/she had to return home on a flight that morning to start school a few days later. Your friend wonders how his/her life would have been different had he/she agreed to do the movie.

Q1. What would you say to console your friend?

Q2. Do you have any advice for your friend about going forward in the future?

Q3. Do you have any similar regrets from your own life?

 Moments You Wish You Could Relive

1. Falling in love
2. Laughing until your stomach hurts
3. Accidentally hearing somebody say something good about you
4. Feel butterflies in your stomach every time you see a certain person
5. Seeing an old friend again and feeling that things have not changed
6. Watching a sunset
7. Hearing a song that makes you remember a special person
8. Walking alone on a silent road at night and listening to your favorite songs
9. Waking up tired and realizing that you can sleep in for a few more hours
10. And the last one is "RIGHT NOW"

Q. If you could relive any moment in your life, what would it be? Decide and then share the best moments in your life.

If I Could Change One Thing

7. Cultural Discussion Questions

Read the passage and talk about the questions in as much detail as possible.

Top 5 Deathbed Regrets

Of all the regrets people have while on their deathbeds, these are the top 5.

First, people wish that they had the courage to live the life they wanted to live, not one expected by others. Many people die without fulfilling even half of the dreams that they've had since childhood.

Second, they wish they had spent less time working and more time doing what they enjoyed, like spending time with their families and pursuing their hobbies and interests.

Third, they wish that they had had the courage to express how they were really feeling. Often, we tend to hide how we are really feeling in order to keep the peace. However, we often develop bitterness or resentment in our hearts if we feel that we are not allowed to be honest about how we feel.

Fourth, they wish they had stayed in touch with their friends.

And **finally,** the fifth most common regret is that they wish they had let themselves be happier in life. Many do not realize that happiness is often a choice, and out of fear of the unknown and the comfort of the familiar, they chose to remain in depressing situations.

1. Do you regret any of the items from the list?
2. Why do you think these regrets are so common?

Balance for a Happy Life

More than 670 US workers were surveyed about their attempts to maintain a balance between their personal and professional lives.

In the workplace, particularly among young single professionals, men are nearly two times more likely than women to balance their work and personal lives. These men are 25% more likely to take breaks throughout the day for personal activities.

Men are consistently happier than women in the office and at home.

+25% at work
+8% at home

75% of men are happy with their work-life balance

compared to 70% of women

The impact of a poor work-life balance can be serious. Nearly 87% of respondents, particularly women, indicated that work-life balance affects their health.

For **87% of men and women**, work-life balance affects their health in a negative way.

STRESS 58% / 67%   HEADACHES 43% / 54%

TENSION 34% / 44%

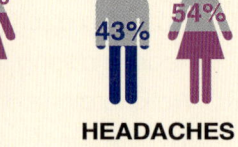
WEIGHT GAIN 37% / 44%

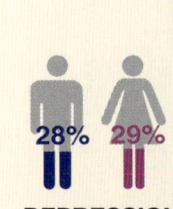
DEPRESSION 28% / 29%

Q1. Do you believe that you have achieved a good balance between your personal life and work? Why or why not?

Q2. What are some things that people can do to live a more balanced life?

8. If You Ask Me

Read the discussion topic and select the statement that you believe in the most. Then role-play the scenario.

Winds of Caution

There are really **two kinds of people** in the world: those **who take the cautious approach to life** and those **who throw caution to the wind and live life to the fullest.** Both options have their benefits and drawbacks. For instance, by being cautious, there could be more chance for stability, success, and predictability in life. There are no great adventures, but there also are not many great tragedies. However, for those who prefer to seize every day, the stable and predictable life is boring, and some even say it is not truly living. For them, if a whim strikes to experience something they have never experienced before, they will follow that whim, whether it leads to great success or complete and utter failure. They will also point out that, sometimes, tragedy also strikes the more cautious, and that life does not always go according to plan.

Topic Question
Do you think it is better to live cautiously or to seize the day and take life as it comes?

Supportive Opinion VS Non-Supportive Opinion

Role-play

Act out the role-play using the slang and idioms and useful expressions.

Situation
You are an aging parent and your partner is your child. He or she has just celebrated a major milestone in his or her life (graduation, wedding, promotion, etc.) and you would like to congratulate him or her. You can't believe how quickly time has passed and you feel regretful that you were unable to be around more when he or she was growing up.

Role A
- Tell your child how you feel.
- Apologize for not spending more time with him or her.

Role B
- Accept your parent's apology.
- Reassure your parent that he or she helped you lead a happy life.

Wrapping Up!
Tell four things that you learned from this lesson and review.

1.
2.
3.
4.

05 International Relations

Learning Objective
Upon completion of this lesson you will be able to **discuss relationships between countries.**

Expression Check

- ☑ Free trade agreements can be mutually beneficial for all countries involved.
- ☑ It's in the best interest of each country to strike an accord.
- ☑ The problem with governments these days is that they're just in it for themselves.

1. Warm Up Activity
Talk about the questions.

1. Do you think having one unified global government would make the world a better place?
2. What would it take for the world to be more peaceful?
3. How would you describe the relationship between your country and its neighboring countries?

2. Useful Phrases
Match the phrases (a-d) to the phrases (1-4) to form a complete sentence. The useful phrases are italicized.

A Free trade agreements

B *It's in the best interest of each country*

C Many officials *have diplomatic immunity*

D *The problem with* governments *these days*

1 to *strike an accord.*

2 is they're just *in it for themselves.*

3 can be mutually beneficial for all countries involved.

4 when visiting other countries.

3. Slang & Idioms

Check out the slang and idioms and try to make your own sentences.

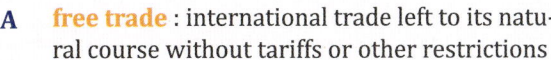

A	**free trade** : international trade left to its natural course without tariffs or other restrictions	Many people are quick to praise the benefits of free trade.
B	**strike an accord** : to make an agreement	The two countries struck an accord at the summit.
C	**diplomatic immunity** : the privilege of exemption from certain laws and taxes granted to diplomats working abroad	The two men claimed diplomatic immunity and were ultimately not charged with any wrongdoing.
D	**hostility** : acts of warfare or other negative diplomatic behavior	Even before the dramatic escalation of hostilities yesterday, people had doubts about the agreement.

4. Key Conversation

 Read through the dialogue and practice with a partner.

Welcome to the Team

Jonathan	Everyone, I would like you to welcome Mr. Chan. He is the visiting representative from our new factory in Cambodia.
Chan	Thank you, Jonathan. Because of the hostilities between our two nations in the past, it has been difficult to strike an accord or to do business with one another.
Jonathan	Yes, that is until recently. Thank goodness.
Chan	My feelings exactly. The problem with governments is that they are just in it for themselves. Meanwhile, the common people want to do business and live our lives.
Jonathan	Is that the reason your company sought a partnership with ours?
Chan	It is. In fact, I think it's in everyone's best interests that we cooperate with one another. Each of us has resources that could benefit the other.
Jonathan	Well then, on behalf of our offices here, we welcome you to our international team.
Chan	Thank you. I expect that this will be a profitable relationship for everyone involved.

Questions

1. How do you think the Cambodian and Canadian offices of the company will benefit from this partnership?

2. Do you think the partnership will set a good example for other companies to follow?

International Relations

Free Trade Benefits

Recently, there has been much debate in the news on whether countries should limit taxes imposed on imports and exports and agree to free trade terms with selected countries around the world.

What are the advantages of a Free Trade Agreement (FTA)?

INCREASE IN PRODUCTIVITY
Free trade enables each country to specialize in producing commodities in which they have a competitive advantage.

EFFICIENT PRODUCTIVITY
Allowing free trade makes the allocation of resources within an economy more efficient. This creates higher productivity and boosts the total output of goods and services.

GAIN IN CONSUMER SURPLUS
Opening up to free trade benefits every consumer as they can now obtain a larger variety of goods and services at lower costs due to increased competition and reductions to the cost of inputs.

ECONOMIC GROWTH
In terms of businesses, free trade rewards risk taking by increasing sales, profits, and market shares.

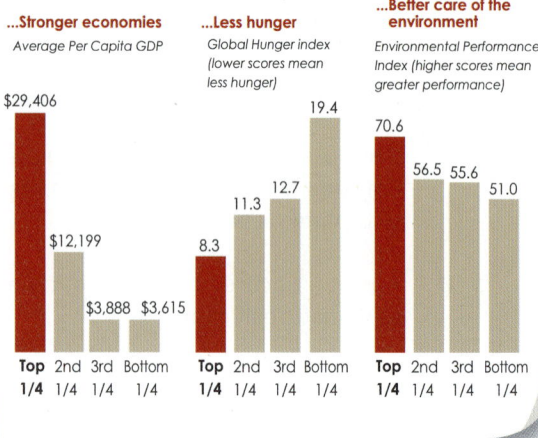

The chart shows that the benefits of free trade are hard to deny. Countries that have more trade freedom also enjoy stronger economies, less hunger, and take better care of the environment.

Q1. Numerous benefits of FTAs are listed above. Can you think of any disadvantages?

Q2. Does your country currently have any FTAs? How have they affected the local economy?

5. Situational Collocations

Complete the sentences using the collocations from the word box.

Word Box

- situation unfolds
- significant misunderstanding
- negotiate peace
- settle the dispute
- sever ties
- through diplomatic channels
- share credit
- reach an agreement

1. The decision to _____ with Turkey took everyone by surprise.
2. I think it's better that we settle this _____.
3. The two leaders met together to _____.
4. I'm surprised the two ambassadors were finally about to _____.
5. The negotiations fell through when she refused to _____ for the idea.
6. There has been a _____ here.
7. We will keep you updated as the _____.
8. Due to his long-standing relationship with the president, he was happy to step in to _____.

6. What Would You Do?

Read the situation and explain what you would do in that situation.

International Transfer

Your supervisor has chosen you to represent the domestic branch of your company at an international conference abroad. Since you work for a global company, there will be representatives from all over the world. You are very proud that your boss has considered you for such a prestigious position. However, if you accept this job, you must also agree to be transferred permanently to a branch office abroad where you will continue to collaborate on international projects. Your family is happy living in your country but has agreed to support you in whatever you choose. You worry about adjusting to life in a foreign country but are also excited about the opportunity to advance your career.

Q1. Would you accept the job?

Q2. How could you help your family adjust to life abroad?

Q3. Would you be interested in working abroad if the opportunity arose?

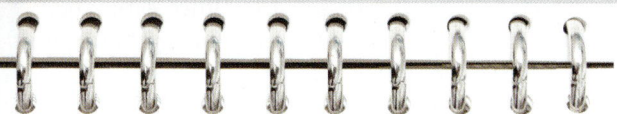
Abolishing Nuclear Weapons

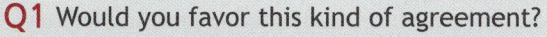

Currently, **44 countries have access to the fissile materials and technology necessary to build nuclear weapons.** With the Nuclear Non-Proliferation Treaty jeopardized, nuclear weapons could quickly spread.
Below are the responses to a survey conducted to find out whether people around the world would favor or oppose an international agreement for eliminating all nuclear weapons.

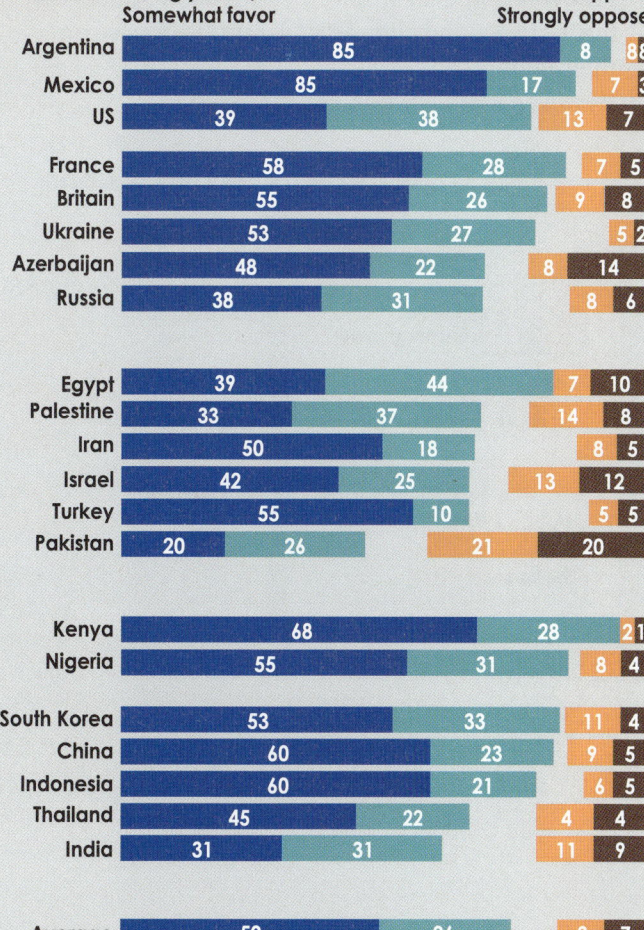

Q1 Would you favor this kind of agreement?

Q2 How would such an agreement affect international relations?

International Relations

7. Cultural Discussion Questions

Read the passage and talk about the questions in as much detail as possible.

Trading Free of Tariffs

In order to protect the interests of local industries, governments often impose special taxes on imported goods known as tariffs. The goal of tariffs is to guarantee that locally priced goods will be more affordable than those produced in foreign markets. By keeping domestic industries profitable, governments can also guarantee the employment and prosperity of their own citizens. However, not everything can be produced locally, so many countries come together with neighboring countries to create free trade agreements, which allow for the import and export of certain goods and services without tariffs.

1. In your opinion, are free trade agreements a good thing or a bad thing?
2. Which products are your country's biggest exports?

Free Trade Agreement Pros & Cons

Free trade agreements are treaties that regulate the tariffs, taxes, and duties that countries impose on their imports and exports.
However, it is always on controversy:

Pros

1. Increased economic growth
The U.S. Trade Representative Office estimates that NAFTA increased U.S. economic growth by 0.5 percent a year.

2. Lower government spending
Many governments subsidize local industry segments. After the trade agreement removes subsidies, those funds can be put to better use.

3. Technology transfer
Local companies also receive access to the latest technologies from their multinational partners.

Cons

1. Increased job outsourcing
Many U.S. manufacturing industries laid off workers as a result of NAFTA.

2. Poor working conditions
Women and children from emerging market countries are often subjected to grueling factory jobs in sub-standard conditions.

3. Degradation of natural resources
Free trade leads to depletion of timber, minerals, and other natural resources.

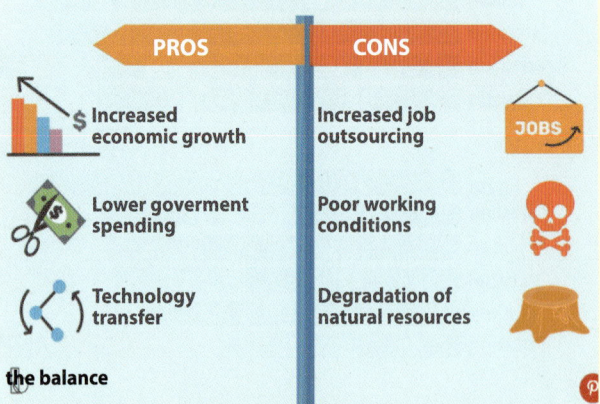

Q1 Why do you think it is important to keep positive international relatives?

Q2 What other advantages or disadvantages of FTA can you think of?

Lesson 05 / International Relations

8. If You Ask Me

Read the discussion topic and select the statement that you believe in the most. Then role-play the scenario.

Diplomatic Immunity

Diplomatic immunity is a policy that allows diplomats and representatives from various countries to visit one another's country without needing to worry about lawsuits or legal issues in the destination country. It is meant to prevent embarrassing international incidents from emerging between two countries. However, some take advantage of this diplomatic immunity and use it to escape prosecution for criminal activities, leading many to feel that diplomats are above the law.

Topic Question

Should diplomats and other government employees working abroad be subject to the same laws as everyone else?

Supportive Opinion VS **Non-Supportive Opinion**

Role-play

Act out the role-play using the slang and idioms and useful expressions.

Situation

You and a co-worker are discussing a recent FTA that your country entered into. You think that the agreement is great because your country will have access to a wider range of goods at a lower price and also be able to export your products to a wider market. Your co-worker is strongly opposed to the agreement because he or she believes it will cost domestic workers their jobs. You feel that your co-worker is not well informed about the topic and needs to learn more before forming an opinion. Try to make your coworker see the benefits.

Role A
- Explain what you know about FTAs.
- Tell your co-worker how you feel about the topic.

Role B
- Insist that the FTA will be bad for local workers.
- Describe how you feel about the situation.

Wrapping Up!

Tell four things that you learned from this lesson and review.

1.
2.
3.
4.

06 Prepping for an Emergency

Learning Objective

Upon completion of this lesson you will be able to **discuss natural disasters and how to prepare for them.**

Expression Check

- ☑ In the event of a...
- ☑ Whatever you do, don't...
- ☑ The first thing you should do during a...

1. Warm Up Activity

Talk about the questions.

1. What are some kinds of natural disasters that you know of?
2. Which natural disasters are common in your country?
3. Do you have an emergency disaster kit? If so, what have you included and why?

2. Useful Phrases

Match the phrases (a-d) to the phrases (1-4) to form a complete sentence. The useful phrases are italicized.

- A The house *was blown away by*
- B The landslide *tore down*
- C The earthquake virtually
- D The rain *poured down*

- 1 all the trees on the mountain.
- 2 for days on end.
- 3 the strong tornado.
- 4 *swallowed up* the village.

3. Slang & Idioms

Check out the slang and idioms and try to make your own sentences.

- **A** **twister** : a tornado — *I couldn't believe it when I saw the twister out the window.*
- **B** **a storm brewing** : extreme weather is coming — *It looks like there is a storm brewing.*
- **C** **blow over** : go away without serious consequences — *The weatherman said the storm front will blow over in a few hours.*
- **D** **flood out** : have to leave one's home because of a flood — *We're holding a fundraiser for the victims who were flooded out of their homes.*

4. Key Conversation

Read through the dialogue and practice with a partner.

Getting Ready

Tim	Hey, Eileen! The weather report says a hurricane is brewing off the coast and is expected to touch land in 48 hours. We'd better get ready. What should I do?
Eileen	Don't worry. I'm always ready. When you've lived here a couple of years, you'll always be ready, too.
Tim	Is that right? So, what do I do first?
Eileen	In the event of a hurricane, you should check to see that you have a supply of non-perishable food, potable water, candles, waterproof matches, first aid kit, fire extinguisher, battery-powered radio, flashlights, and extra batteries. Oh, and don't forget a stash of cash.
Tim	Wow! You really are organized!
Eileen	You can be, too. Just stick by me during this hurricane, keep your eyes and ears open, and you'll learn all you need to know. Knowing the do's and don'ts during a hurricane can be a question of life or death.
Tim	OK, OK!! Go on… what else should I know?
Eileen	The first thing you should do before a hurricane hits is go to the nearest hurricane shelter and stay put until you're informed by those in charge that it's safe to leave.
Tim	I see. So, do you know where the nearest shelter is?
Eileen	Well… we have one right here in the building….

Questions
1. Do you think Eileen has experienced a hurricane before?
2. Do you think Eileen's advice is good?

Prepping for an Emergency

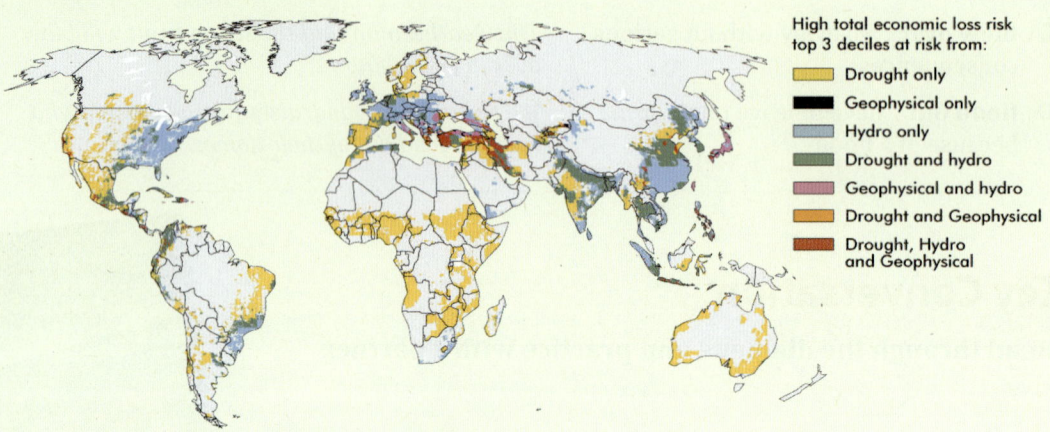

This map represents an analysis of exposure to hazards and the historical vulnerability of selected natural disasters, together with population distribution and economic factors.

 Have you ever been in a natural disaster? If so, what did you learn from it? If not, have you ever practiced to protect yourself from a natural disaster?

5. Situational Collocations

Complete the sentences using the collocations from the word box.

Word Box

- inclement weather
- seek shelter
- storm clouds
- disaster relief
- heavy rain
- emergency preparedness
- emergency exit
- automated alert

1. Our office held an _____ drill to get everyone ready for tornado season.
2. In the event of a tornado, you are advised to _____ and stay inside.
3. I had a bad feeling as I watched the _____ approaching.
4. An _____ was sent out to warn people of the approaching storm.
5. The _____ forced the team to cancel their game.
6. Always make sure you know where the _____ is in case of fire.
7. The president sent in _____ teams to help people after the hurricane.
8. The _____ has kept us out of the garden today.

6. What Would You Do?

Read the situation and explain what you would do in that situation.

To Open or Not to Open

You and your friend are staying in a mountain cabin over the weekend. There has just been an emergency announcement warning that there are tornadoes in the area. Your friend is convinced that it is absolutely necessary to open all the windows because air pressure differences could cause the house to explode if a tornado comes near. You know that people used to believe this in the past, but science has proven this just to be a myth. You feel that opening the windows is riskier than leaving them closed.

Q1. What would you say to convince your friend to close the windows without hurting his feelings?

Q2. What would you do if your friend refuses to accept what you told him as the truth?

Q3. How would you prepare for a tornado?

How Much Do Natural Disasters Cost?

Disasters can be particularly notable for the high costs associated with responding to and recovering from them.

For instance, the costliest natural disaster in the recorded history is **The Tohoku earthquake which triggered a tsunami** on March 11, 2011. More than 450,000 people became homeless as a result of the tsunami. More than 15,500 people died. The tsunami also severely crippled the infrastructure of the country. In addition to the thousands of destroyed homes, businesses, roads, and railways, the tsunami caused the meltdown of three nuclear reactors at the Fukushima Daiichi Nuclear Power Plant. Below is a chart of the Top Ten Costliest Natural Disasters:

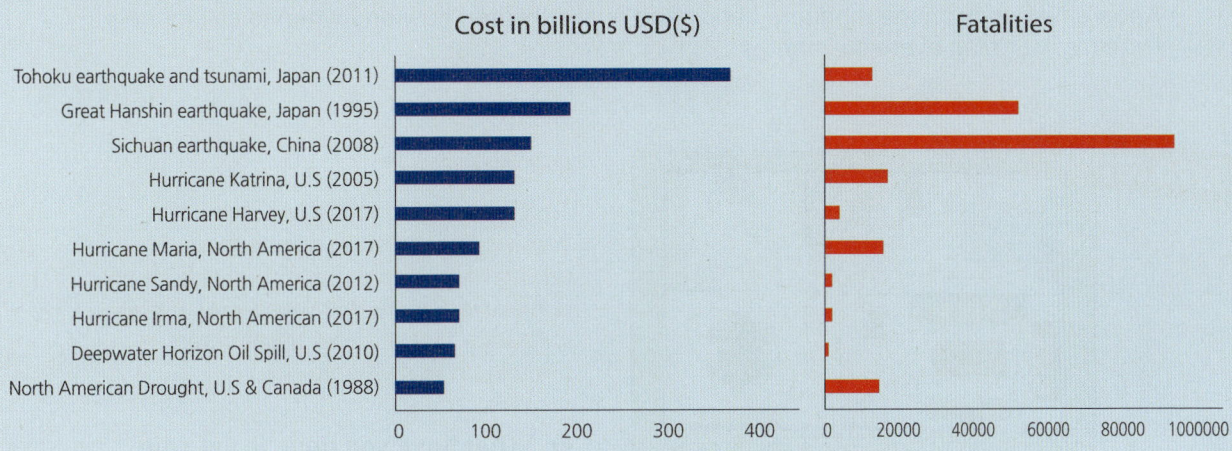

Q1. What was the costliest disaster that occurred in your country?

Q2. Where do you think is the safest place to live if you want to avoid a natural disaster?

Prepping for an Emergency

7. Cultural Discussion Questions

Read the passage and talk about the questions in as much detail as possible.

"We Are Interrupting This Program for a Special News Bulletin....."

Modern day methods of mass communication have given us the means to spread information vital to public safety. In the US, local television and radio stations interrupt broadcasting to give warnings concerning local disasters. Some areas also operate emergency sirens or post emergency service workers with megaphones to warn the public of inclement weather.

1. In your country, where is the best place to look for information about possible natural disasters?
2. In your opinion, can all natural disasters be predicted?

What If Nobody Comes to Help?

First, You Need an Emergency Survival Kit!

Your survival kit should include:
- First, aid items for your home and vehicle: band-aids, tweezers, scissors, thermometer, safety pins, rubbing alcohol or antiseptic wipes, disposable gloves, sunscreen, soap or hand sanitizer
- Extra clothing and bedding to keep warm
- Important documents
- Games and books to help pass the time

Second, Make a Family Disaster Plan

- Create evacuation plans with your family in case of a disaster.
- Establish an out-of-area contact that each person can check in with.
- Keep emergency phone numbers handy and teach children how and when to call for help.
- Practice your plan every six months.

Example

Did you know?

Text messaging is the best way to communicate during a widespread emergency. Phone calls require a direct connection while text messages travel in "bursts" that can be transmitted as bandwidth is available.

Q. What have you done to get your family prepared for a natural disaster?

Lesson 06 / Prepping for an Emergency

8. If You Ask Me

Read the discussion topic and select the statement that you believe in the most. Then role-play the scenario.

"…But I Don't Know What to Do…"

Most people have participated in emergency "drills" or "practice runs" to know what to do in the case of an impending natural disaster. Those practices contribute to helping people keep calm during an emergency situation as well. Some go as far as to organize drills of this kind with their family in the home. In some areas, this is a common practice – even recommended by local authorities. Others claim this to be a waste of time and say it might also annoy the neighbors, especially if the family lives in an apartment building.

Topic Question

Do you think it is a good idea to organize "drills" of this kind in your home?

Supportive Opinion VS Non-Supportive Opinion

Role-play

Act out the role-play using the slang and idioms and useful expressions.

Situation

You have been chosen to transfer to a branch of your company in Kansas for three years. You are happy and excited about the prospect of living and working in the US. However, Kansas is known for tornadoes, and you are terrified about the possibility of experiencing terrible, life-threatening tornadoes while you are there. You tell your friend, who has been to Kansas, and ask how to tell when a twister is brewing as well as how to protect yourself.

Role A
- Explain why you are worried.
- Ask for your friend's help.

Role B
- Tell your friend to check for warnings on local television.
- Suggest that your friend avoid windows and stay inside.

Wrapping Up!

Tell four things that you learned from this lesson and review.

1.
2.
3.
4.

07 Our Top Story Tonight

Learning Objective
Upon completion of this lesson you will be able to **discuss headline news and current events.**

Expression Check

- ☑ Did you happen to catch the evening news and hear about...?
- ☑ It's hard to believe something so tragic could actually happen.
- ☑ This story will certainly spark a lot of debate.

1. Warm Up Activity

Talk about the questions.

1. Do you think it is important for people to be up-to-date on the news? Why or why not?
2. How do you get the news?
3. What different categories of news stories do you know of? Which are the most interesting to you?

2. Useful Phrases

Match the phrases (a-d) to the phrases (1-4) to form a complete sentence. The useful phrases are italicized.

A. This story will certainly

B. There *was a public outcry*

C. He's been working hard

D. She claimed that the news of the incident was

1. *to meet the deadline.*
2. *fresh off the press.*
3. *when the scandal first broke.*
4. *spark a lot of debate.*

3. Slang & Idioms

Check out the slang and idioms and try to make your own sentences.

A	**breaking news** : newly received information about an event that is currently occurring	*This site is the best place for breaking news on technology and the Internet.*
B	**scoop** : a piece of news published by a newspaper or broadcast by a television station before its rivals	*Since I revealed the big scoop, I have had it reconfirmed by yet another highly authoritative source.*
C	**fresh off the wire** : newly released news; usually sensational and exciting	*Listen to this story — it's fresh off the wire!*
D	**off the record** : not made as an official or attributable statement	*This is off the record, but I disagree with the mayor on this matter.*

4. Key Conversation

🎧 **Read through the dialogue and practice with a partner.**

Breaking News

Jack	Hi! Did you hear what happened last night? There was a shooting in the Westbrooke Shopping Mall!
Steve	Yes, we were watching a movie on TV, and they interrupted the program and announced the incident. How terrible!
Jack	I know. It was the top story on the local news this morning. They say they don't know yet how many people have been killed, if any, but at least 15 people have been hospitalized in critical condition. Have they caught anyone yet?
Steve	I heard that they don't even know if there was one shooter or two.
Jack	Can you imagine doing your weekly shopping and suddenly there are bullets flying everywhere?
Steve	Well, I'm glad I wasn't there. I had been there earlier. But… it was a Friday night… there were a lot of families with small children there doing their weekend shopping. What a tragedy!
Jack	This story will certainly spark a lot of debate about gun laws.
Steve	Yes, it most definitely will! In the living rooms as well as on TV.
Jack	Let's check online to see if there have been any updates.

1. Do you think that Jack watches the news often?
2. Do you think the men agree with the current gun laws?

Our Top Story Tonight

Media Consolidation The Illusion of Choice

Media has never been more consolidated. 6 MEDIA GIANTS now control a staggering **90%** of what we read, watch, or listen to.

CONSOLIDATION

In 1983, 90% of American media was owned by 50 companies.

In 2017, that same 90% is controlled by just 6 companies.

THE SIX COMPANIES ARE

Comcast
Holdings include:
NBC
Universal Pictures
DreamWorks Animation

The Walt Disney Company
Holdings include:
ABC
ESPN
Marvel Entertainment
Pixar

AT&T
Holdings include:
Warner Media
HBO
CNN

21st Century Fox
Holdings include:
The Fox Broadcasting Company
Fox News
National Geographic

CBS Corporation
Holdings include:
CBS
Showtime
Entercom
Simon & Schuster

Viacom
Holdings include:
MTX
Nickelodeon
Paramount Pictures

Q. What are some advantages and disadvantages of media consolidation?

5. Situational Collocations

Complete the sentences using the collocations from the word box.

Word Box

- gauge the reaction
- heavily debated
- disseminate fake news
- eyewitness reports
- make the news
- declining circulation
- broadcast journalism
- gain publicity

❶ In recent years, newspapers have struggled with _____.

❷ This is our pilot project to _____ of users before launching.

❸ I think _____, by and large, does not do a very good job.

❹ He later admitted that he engineered the incident in an effort to _____.

❺ The scandal has quickly become one of the most _____ stories of the year.

❻ According to _____, the woman collapsed shortly after arriving.

❼ Positive stories don't often _____.

❽ The president has called on people urging them not to _____.

6. What Would You Do?

Read the situation and explain what you would do in that situation.

What's in the News?

Many people believe that keeping up with current events is important. You have two children and consider education to be the most important things in their lives. To eliminate things that could distract them from their studies, you do not have a television in your home, limit their access to things like newspapers and magazines, and restrict their time on the Internet. However, you would like to instill in your children the importance of keeping up-to-date on important news from around the world.

Q1. How would you ensure that your children are learning about current events?

Q2. How could you allow your children access to information without giving them complete freedom?

Q3. Do you believe that children should be allowed to control certain aspects of their own schedules? Why or why not?

Highly Educated People Watch More News

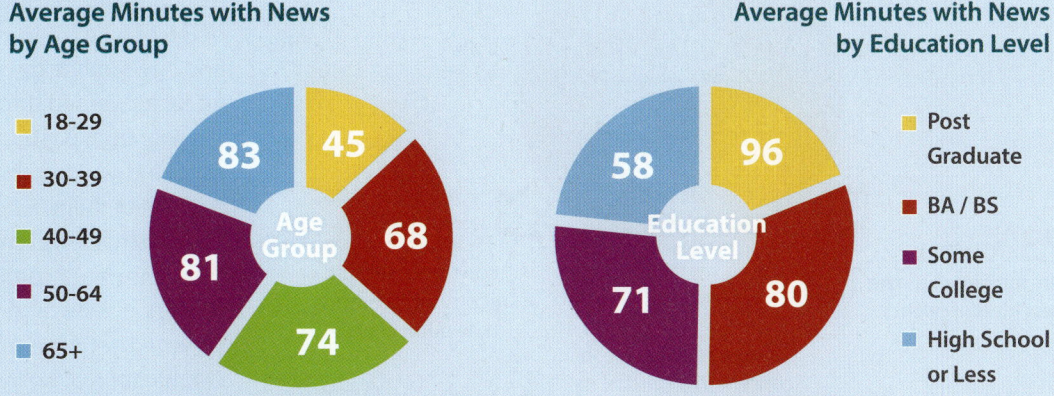

Average Minutes with News by Age Group
- 18-29: 45
- 30-39: 68
- 40-49: 74
- 50-64: 81
- 65+: 83

Average Minutes with News by Education Level
- Post Graduate: 96
- BA / BS: 80
- Some College: 71
- High School or Less: 58

The groups that are driving the rise in news consumption are mainly well-educated people, who are likely to view news on both digital and traditional platforms.

Q. What form of media do you usually go to for your daily news? How often do you check the news?

Our Top Story Tonight

7. Cultural Discussion Questions

Read the passage and talk about the questions in as much detail as possible.

What's the Hotline Number?

Have you ever wondered how the press always seems to be on the scene when something exciting happens? Sometimes it seems like they even reach an accident before the police and rescue teams do. Many television stations feel like they need to get a "scoop" in order to stay ahead of the competition. With this in mind, they advertise a toll-free number that people can use to report crimes and other newsworthy events. Usually, the first person that reports something will receive a monetary reward.

1. Do your local TV news channels have a website where you can report or follow up on a news story?
2. Is there a police hotline in your country? When do people use it?

Social Networks and the News

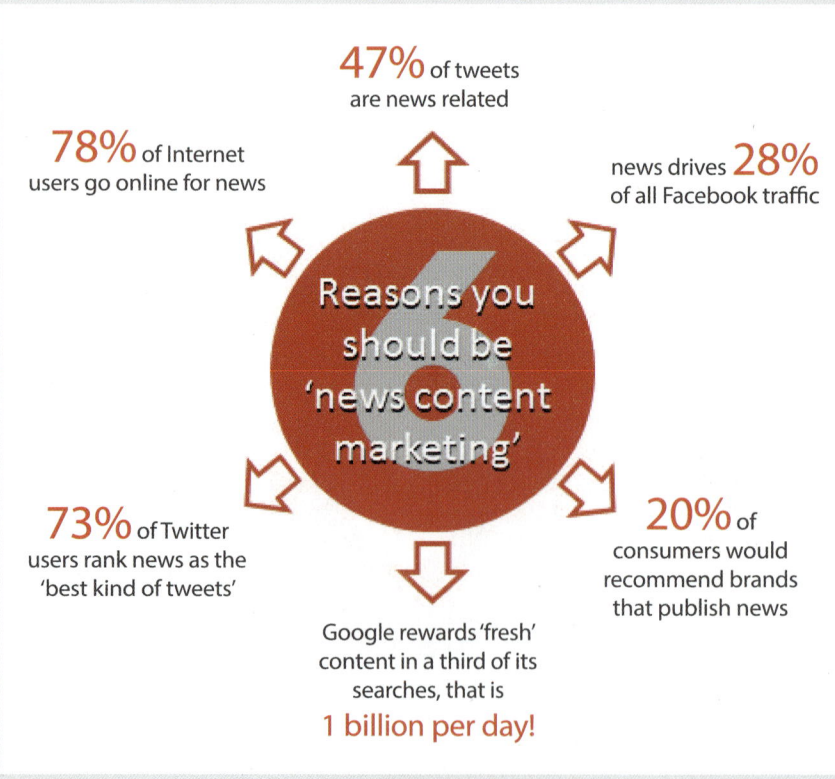

The latest study from Pew Internet analyzes the news Americans are consuming and the various ways they find news. Based on a sample of 2,259 adults, the study reveals that three-fourths of the people (75%) who find news online get it either forwarded through email or from posts on social networking sites, and half of them (52%) forward the news through those means. According to the report, 59% of those surveyed get news from a combination of online and offline sources.

 How often do you find or share news through social media platforms?

Lesson 07 / Our Top Story Tonight 51

8. If You Ask Me

Read the discussion topic and select the statement that you believe in the most. Then role-play the scenario.

The News: On or Offline?

In this day and age of mass media, there are so many different ways to keep informed of the news. Some would argue that the best way to keep up with the top news is via the Internet, which is updated quickly and gives more details than television. With all the newer wireless devices, the Internet can be consulted anywhere at any time. Others claim the best way to get news is still from television broadcasts and the newspaper. TV stations report stories quickly and in condensed forms that are perfect for those who are short on time, while the newspaper offers high-quality journalism in a form that is just as portable as a smartphone.

Topic Question

Do you think that online news can truly replace old standards like television news and newspapers?

Supportive Opinion VS **Non-Supportive Opinion**

Role-play

Act out the role-play using the slang and idioms and useful expressions.

Situation

You and your friend are discussing recent headline news stories over lunch. On the morning news, you watched a report about a 26-car pileup on an expressway outside the city. At least 12 people died in the high-speed crash with 10 more taken to the hospital with life-threatening injuries. The accident makes you think that you will start driving more carefully. Your friend didn't hear about the incident yet and is interested in learning more details.

Role A
- Tell your friend about what you saw on the news.
- Ask how it makes your friend feel.

Role B
- Comment with your opinion of the accident.
- Say that you will look it up later.

Wrapping Up!

Tell four things that you learned from this lesson and review.

1. _____ 2. _____ 3. _____ 4. _____

08 Moving On From a Setback

Learning Objective

Upon completion of this lesson you will be able to **handle and react to personal and professional setbacks.**

Expression Check

- ☑ I'm turning the page—this is a new chapter in my life.
- ☑ On to bigger and better things.
- ☑ I'm just taking life one day at a time.

1. Warm Up Activity

Talk about the questions.

1. Do you believe in second chances? Why or why not?
2. Do you believe that holding on to the past hinders you from moving forward?
3. Do you think it is easy to pick up and move on without looking back?

2. Useful Phrases

Match the phrases (a-d) to the phrases (1-4) to form a complete sentence. The useful phrases are italicized.

A. Changing careers seems like *a big risk to take*, but

B. I'm ready for a change.

C. It was a huge setback, but

D. Things have been rough lately, so

1. I'm *taking it day by day*.
2. I'm *picking up the pieces* and moving on.
3. I've got to *follow my heart*.
4. It's *time for me to shed my old skin*.

3. Slang & Idioms

Check out the slang and idioms and try to make your own sentences.

A	**out with the old, in with the new** : to leave old things or ideas behind and start fresh with new ones	It's time to move on. You know what they say "Out with the old, in with the new."
B	**a new lease on life** : a substantially improved chance at leading a happy or successful life	Moving to another city gave him a new lease on life.
C	**with a clean slate** : start again with a fresh beginning, unencumbered by regrets from the past	I'm ready to start over with a clean slate.
D	**turn the page** : make a fresh start	It feels like I'm turning the page to a new chapter of my life.

4. Key Conversation

 Read through the dialogue and practice with a partner.

" Empty Nest "

James	Well, I think this is the last one.
Lee	You sure have a lot of boxes, little brother. I can't believe you're really going through with this.
James	You know, I'm not getting any younger. I really need to venture out and spread my wings.
Lee	You're right about that, but do you have to spread your wings so far away?
James	It isn't that far. Besides, I want to start with a completely clean slate, and I don't plan on looking back.
Lee	Well, hopefully you'll look back every now and then to check in on those who've gotten you this far.
James	Of course I will. You'll have to come visit me the first chance you get.
Lee	I'll be making sure that you're walking the straight-and-narrow.
James	Oh, most definitely!

1. Do you think it sounds like James is making a wise decision about moving away?
2. Does it seem like Lee and James have a close relationship?

Moving On From a Setback

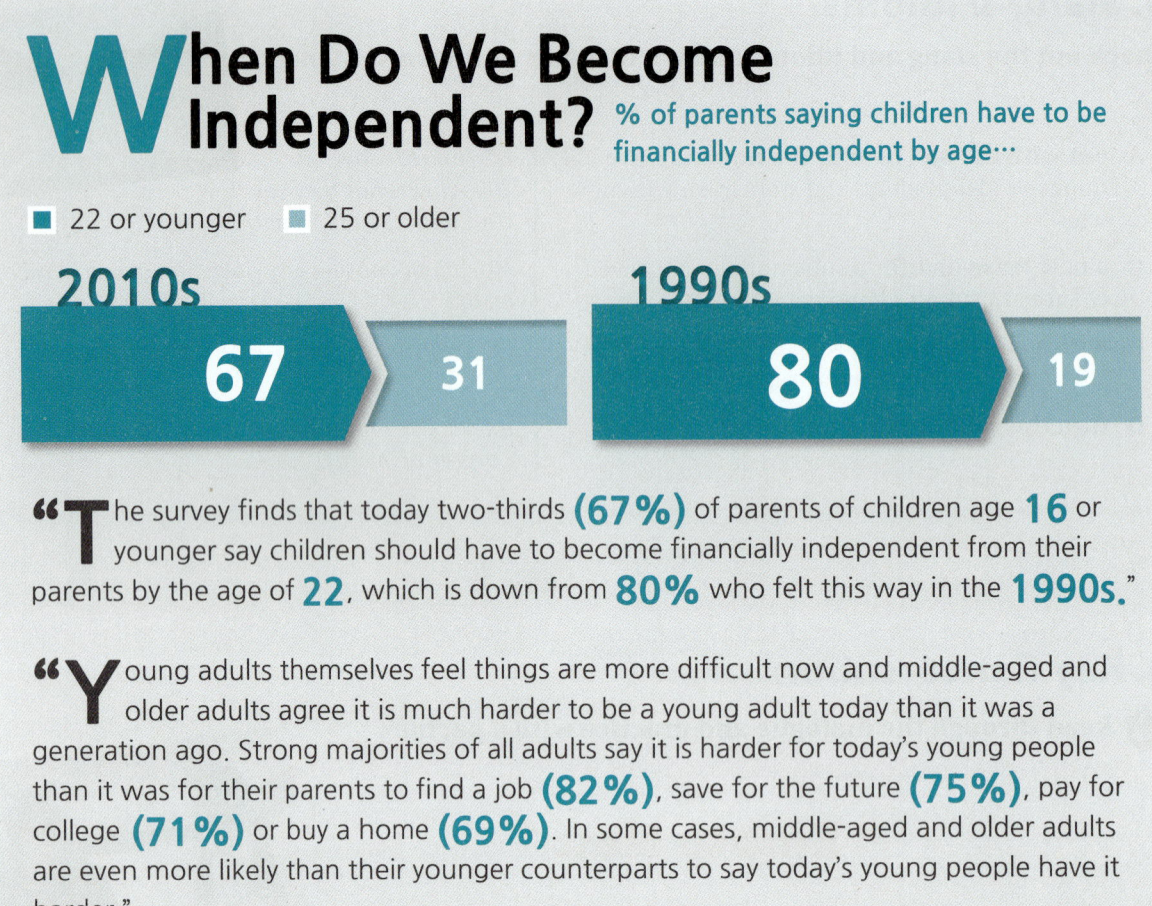

5. Situational Collocations

Complete the sentences using the collocations from the word box.

Word Box
- reassess your decision
- dwell on this problem
- start over
- inevitable conclusion
- minimize the damage
- step forward
- bound to end up
- lingering concerns

1. I figure starting over in a new place is the easiest way to _____.
2. Put your past behind you and _____.
3. This was just the _____ to everything that has happened lately.
4. If you take a chance, you are _____ in a better situation than this.
5. His parents still have _____ that he is going to be able to make it on his own.
6. This is a very progressive and important _____.
7. You shouldn't _____ any longer. What's done is done.
8. I hope you will _____ and stay at our company.

6. What Would You Do?

Read the situation and explain what you would do in that situation.

Should I Stay or Should I Go?

The company you work for recently announced that they are closing their doors where you live. Now, you will have to make some important decisions about your future. The company has offered to relocate you to Europe for a similar position at a substantial pay cut. On one hand, you will not have to seek employment elsewhere.
On the other, you will have to uproot your family and your home. You are trying to remain positive, but you cannot help but worry.

Q1. Who would you go to for advice on this situation?

Q2. What would you like to do?

Q3. In this situation, what seems safer: making a fresh start at a new company or in a new place (Europe)? Explain.

The Power of Now

PAST / PRESENT / FUTURE All negativity is caused by a denial of the present.

Living in the FUTURE causes: Unease, anxiety, tension, stress, worry, dissatisfaction, frustration, which are all forms of fear. The future represents your fulfillment and creates inner conflict when you want what you do not have and do not want what you do have.

Living in the PAST causes: Guilt, regret, resentment, sadness, anger, self-pity, bitterness, which are all forms of non-forgiveness. The past represents your identity and reinforces a false sense of self. It keeps you stuck in "your story" and reduces your quality of life.

Living in the PRESENT causes: Joy, ease, lightness, peace. The present represents "being."

> As you know, the past is EXPERIENCE, Present is EXPERIMENT, and Future is EXPECTATION. Use your EXPERIENCES in your EXPERIMENTS to achieve your EXPECTATIONS.

Q1. What are the advantages of living in the present? How could you apply this to your everyday life?

Moving On From a Setback

7. Cultural Discussion Questions

Read the passage and talk about the questions in as much detail as possible.

Leaving the Nest

In comparison to other mammals, humans keep their children close to them for much longer than is physically necessary for survival. In some cultures, children leave the nest after finishing school, while in others they move out upon marriage. Further yet, it is customary in some cultures for children to invite their parents to move in with them after they have established their own home.

1. When do people usually move out in your culture? Why?
2. At your current age, what do you think is the most comfortable living arrangement between you and your parents? Explain your reasoning.

The Cost of a Satisfying Life

It is one of the most pondered questions of all time – can money buy happiness? The answer, according to a study, is **"YES"** – but so can friendships and successful relationships.

WHAT BUYS YOU JOY... AND WHAT DOES NOT

MEETING FRIENDS AND RELATIVES

Most days: **worth $63,833 a year**

Once or twice a week: **$50,500 a year**

Once or twice a month: **$35,000 a year**

RELATIONSHIPS

Living with someone: **$82,500 a year**

Marriage: **$53,833 a year**

BREAK-UPS

Widowed: **minus $200,000 a year**

Separated: **minus $57,667 a year**

Divorced: **minus $24,500 a year**

CHATTING TO NEIGHBORS REGULARLY

$40,000 a year

HEALTH

Excellent: **$304,000 a year**

Good: **$251,000 a year**

POOR HEALTH

Serious illness: **minus $480,000 a year**

Major disability: **minus $165,000 a year**

* Figures are based on a life satisfaction scale. This represents the same satisfaction as earning that amount of money as a rise in annual salary.

8. If You Ask Me

Read the discussion topic and select the statement that you believe in the most. Then role-play the scenario.

Too Much Information

Living in the Information Age, we are able to search and find almost any information we want with the simple touch of the button. With the rise of social networking services, this also means our personal information. Occasionally, things get posted that we might not want others coming across later. Furthermore, the increased availability of information means that it is more and more difficult to move on and start over with a clean slate.

Topic Question

Do you think that having easy access to information makes it more difficult to truly get a fresh start?

Supportive Opinion

VS

Non-Supportive Opinion

Role-play

Act out the role-play using the slang and idioms and useful expressions.

Situation

You are preparing to move to a new city for a fresh start at an interesting new startup company. This will be the first time you will be apart from your friends and family. Although it will be a sacrifice, you are willing to take the risk so that you can take further your career and grow as a person. You are very excited about your decision, but your best friend is worried about you. Reassure your friend that you are confident in your choice and that it won't be a mistake.

Role A
- Explain why you want to move.
- Reassure your friend that nothing will change in your current relationship.

Role B
- Tell how much you will miss your friend.
- Say you worry that it will be hard to keep in touch.

Wrapping Up! Tell four things that you learned from this lesson and review.

1. 2. 3. 4.

09 I Downloaded It Last Night

Learning Objective
Upon completion of this lesson you will be able to **share your opinion on media sharing and downloads.**

Expression Check
- ☑ I found this great website for downloading music and movies.
- ☑ The problem with this is the artist is cut out of any royalties.
- ☑ I have no qualms about downloading movies off the Internet.

1. Warm Up Activity

Talk about the questions.

1. Describe your personal media library. What kind of music and movies do you have in your collection?
2. Have you ever used the Internet to download media? If so, what are your favorite sources for music and movies?
3. Are there any risks associated with downloading movies or other media in your country? Explain.

2. Useful Phrases

Match the phrases (a-d) to the phrases (1-4) to form a complete sentence. The useful phrases are italicized.

A. I *found this great website for*

B. The problem with this is the artist is

C. I *have no qualms about*

D. The group *will hardly see a dime from this album anyway,*

1. cut out of any royalties.
2. taking a few days off at work.
3. so why should I care?
4. downloading music and movies.

3. Slang & Idioms

Check out the slang and idioms and try to make your own sentences.

A	**anti-piracy laws** : laws aimed at reducing the illegal download of media	Don't you worry about anti-piracy laws when you are downloading songs?
B	**elevator music** : boring background music for stores and other public places	I can't stand the constant elevator music in this coffee shop.
C	**file sharing** : using a computer network to provide information to others	Do you have a file sharing site that you recommend?
D	**strike a chord** : affect or stir someone's emotions	That song really strikes a chord with people of my generation.

4. Key Conversation

Read through the dialogue and practice with a partner.

I Found This Great Website

Chase	Hey Patricia, I see you've got a pretty sweet new MP3 player. What kind of music are you into these days anyway?
Patricia	I've been all over the place lately trying out new things. I found this great website for downloading music and movies, and it's got all the latest tracks from everyone on the charts. I'm not 100% sure it's legal, though. I'm just saying…
Chase	Well, I've got no qualms about downloading stuff off the Internet. The artists will hardly see a dime from their albums anyway, so why should I care? I don't want my hard-earned money going to stuff the pockets of some big corporate execs who couldn't care less about anything other than a top 40 hit.
Patricia	Yeah, the only thing that I feel kind of guilty about is that the artist is cut out of any royalties. But I guess they have to keep up with the times as well.
Chase	Agreed. Hey, speaking of new music, have you had a chance to check out the new track Bassnectar dropped last week?
Patricia	Huh? Who's that? So, what have you got on your playlist for the week?

Questions

1. Do you think Chase and Patricia have the same taste in music?
2. Do you agree with Chase and Patricia about downloading music from the Internet?

I Downloaded It Last Night

Illegal vs. Legal Downloads

One European government introduced regulations a few years ago enabling Internet providers to track users who downloaded illegal content from the web and disable their connection if warning letters had no effect.

It seems like downloading contents from a file-sharing website has been put on par with crimes like class A drugs, people smuggling and human trafficking, major gun crime, fraud and money laundering.

● **Types of illegal downloads**

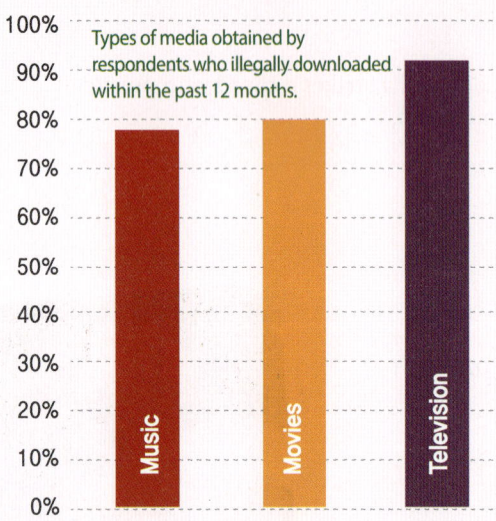

Types of media obtained by respondents who illegally downloaded within the past 12 months.

● **How much would you pay for a legal equivalent?**

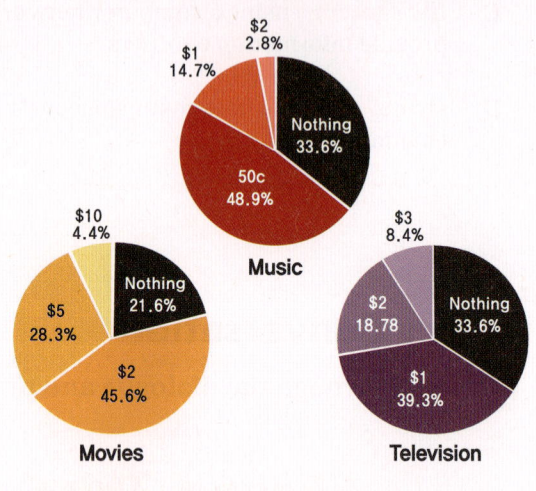

Q. Would you be willing to pay to download files legally?

5. Situational Collocations

Complete the sentences using the collocations from the word box.

Word Box

| · available for download | · click a link | · victimless crime | · streaming a video |
| · time-consuming process | · hack into | · violating the law | · launched its service |

1. Waiting for a file to download is a _____.
2. Most people don't even realize they are _____.
3. A programmer had managed to _____ some top-secret government data.
4. The new media website _____ last Tuesday.
5. Sometimes _____ is more annoying than just downloading it.
6. I'm not so sure that downloading is the _____ that most people think it is.
7. All you need to do to get started is just _____.
8. The movie is _____ in the app store.

How People Spend Their Time Online

● **Percentage of Worldwide Internet Hours by All Users**

● **Average Hours Spent Online Per Person**

INDIA 00:24 /day   CHINA 00:27 /day   USA 01:11 /day   CANADA 01:27 /day

Did You Know?

People age **55** and older represent the **fastest growing** segment of social media users.

Facebook accounted for **1 in every 7 minutes** spent online.

Q1. How do you spend your time when you are online?

Q2. What kind of information do you share with your friends online?

6. What Would You Do?

Read the situation and explain what you would do in that situation.

A Tempting Conclusion to a Foreign Trilogy

You have gotten wind of the release of the final part of a movies series from another country that you really want to watch. You know it will not be out in your country for at least a year due to legalities and translation issues. That is not a problem for a big fan like you, though, because you know where you can download a fansub version of it already online. You are tempted to have a viewing party with a few of your close friends who are also huge fans.

Q1. Would you feel bad about breaking the law?

Q2. What would you say to invite your friends to your party?

Q3. If you downloaded the movie now, would you still want to spend money seeing it on the big screen later?

I Downloaded It Last Night

7. Cultural Discussion Questions

Read the passage and talk about the questions in as much detail as possible.

Musicians on Music

Musicians must decide for themselves how to cope with the spread of file sharing sites and the illegal distribution of their creative work. Some artists have decided to use digital music as a way to promote their shows, offering their material for free. These musicians might offer teaser tracks or even whole albums for download as a way of combating music piracy, choosing to raise ticket prices to compensate for the loss of income from the albums. Others offer special edition covers or other unique features and contests to entice superfans and collectors to continue buying copies of their albums.

1. What do recording artists in your country have to say about the surge in illegal downloads, and how are they adjusting their marketing or distribution tactics?
2. Do you think a musician should be paid for each song he or she makes? Why or why not?

How Much Do You Spend on the Web?

Nearly 65% of Internet users have paid to download or access some kind of online content from the Internet.

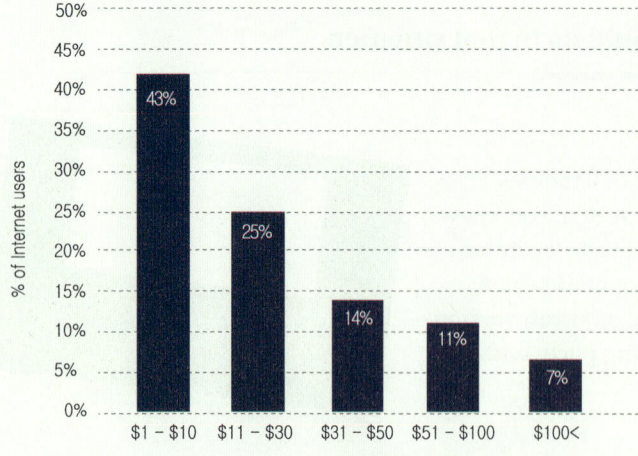

Money spent for online content in a given month

Here is what they have paid for:

33% of Internet users have paid for digital music online
33% have paid for software
21% have paid for apps for their cell phones or tablet computers
19% have paid for digital games
18% have paid for digital newspapers, magazines, or journal articles or reports
16% have paid for videos, movies, or TV shows
15% have paid for ringtones
12% have paid for digital photos
11% have paid for members-only premium content from a website that has other free material on it
10% have paid for e-books
7% have paid for podcasts
5% have paid for tools or materials to use in video or computer games
5% have paid for "cheats or codes" to help them in video games
5% have paid to access particular websites such as online dating sites or services
2% have paid for adult content

Q1. Have you ever paid to download something? What was it?

Q2. How much do you spend on online contents in a month?

Lesson 09 / I Downloaded It Last Night   63

8. If You Ask Me

Read the discussion topic and select the statement that you believe in the most. Then role-play the scenario.

Old School vs. Digital Media

In this day and age, many people are moving their media libraries away from physical discs and CDs and are going all digital. Some people are purists who believe the quality of the music or video is better with media you can actually hold in your hands. They find pleasure in getting good deals by rummaging through discards at used shops as people unload outdated formats. Others prefer the convenience of having an entire portable media library at their fingertips, ready to go at the push of a button.

Topic Question

Do you prefer to buy physical copies of albums or would you rather have the content in a digital format?

Role-play

Act out the role-play using the slang and idioms and useful expressions.

Situation

You and a friend made plans to watch a movie this weekend, but you discovered the same movie on a website available to download for free. You would rather save the money and invite your friend to enjoy the movie in the privacy of your home. In your opinion, it would be much more comfortable than sitting in a crowded theater. You could even use the money you are saving on the tickets to order in delivery food. You told your friend about your brilliant idea but he or she worries about watching illegal content.

Role A
- Tell your friend about your idea.
- Assure your friend that it is a victimless crime.

Role B
- Explain why you don't want to watch the movie illegally.
- Try to get your friend to agree to go to the theater.

Wrapping Up! Tell four things that you learned from this lesson and review.

1   2   3   4

10 Travel Delays

Learning Objective
Upon completion of this lesson you will be able to **handle missing a scheduled flight.**

Expression Check
- ☑ I missed my flight. Do you have another one available before 3:00?
- ☑ I'm sorry, but the flight has been overbooked. I can offer you a seat on the next one.
- ☑ Is it possible for my baggage to be checked through to my final destination?

1. Warm Up Activity
Talk about the questions.

1. Have you ever missed a scheduled flight or train?
2. Has your luggage ever been lost in transit or delayed to a later flight?
3. Have you ever been stuck in an airport or train station because your flight or train was delayed?

2. Useful Phrases
Match the phrases (a-d) to the phrases (1-4) to form a complete sentence. The useful phrases are italicized.

- A I *missed my flight.*
- B I'm sorry, but the *flight has been overbooked.*
- C Is it possible for my baggage
- D With this delay,

- 1 to be *checked through* to my final destination?
- 2 I can offer you a seat on the next one.
- 3 how am I going to *make my connection*?
- 4 Do you have another one available before 3:00?

3. Slang & Idioms

Check out the slang and idioms and try to make your own sentences.

- **A bumped up / down** : be changed from the seat you paid for to another class

  We were overjoyed when we found out that we got bumped up to business class.

- **B red-eye** : an overnight flight

  I decided to take the red-eye back to give me an extra day at the resort.

- **C layover** : a period of rest or waiting before the next stage in a journey

  I only have a 40-minute layover, so I'm going to have to run to catch my connecting flight.

- **D jetlag** : extreme tiredness felt by a person after a long flight across several time zones

  Despite a cold and jetlag, she still managed to give an amazing presentation.

4. Key Conversation

Read through the dialogue and practice with a partner.

The Day I've Been Having

You wouldn't believe the day I've been having. First of all, there was some kind of emergency at LAX, so my initial flight was delayed by more than an hour and a half on the tarmac.

So, by the time I got here to O'Hare, my connecting flight was already preparing to take off. Suffice to say, I missed my flight out of Chicago and had to check in again for a new boarding pass. And just my luck, all of the flights today are overbooked except for a red-eye that will put me in London at 4 a.m. tomorrow, just three hours before I'm supposed to do my presentation.

Oh well. At least they bumped me up to executive class because the economy and business were already full.
At least now I can get some shut eye during the flight.

* LAX: Los Angeles International Airport

Questions
1. Do you think that it was this man's fault that he missed his connecting flight?
2. What do you think the man will do during his layover?

Travel Delays

8 Ways to Make the Most of Your Layover

Flights with layovers are often cheaper than direct flights. Here are some ideas for how to spend your time during your layover.

1 Work Out
A few minutes of deep breathing and stretching is a fantastic way to work out.

2 Sleep
A few travelers think sleeping in an airport is bad, while others have no qualms about catching some Z's on a terminal bench.

3 Get a Room
Consider paying for short-term lodging.

4 Play a Game
Pack a game or two in your carry-on and get someone waiting in your terminal to play with you.

5 Play an Instrument
A guy who led stranded travelers in a sing-along at Newark Airport became a hero (and a YouTube sensation).

6 Chat with a Stranger
Talk to someone waiting near your gate.

7 Eat
A few airport eateries offer gourmet cuisine.

8 People Watch
Lots of big cities are famed for their people-watching opportunities.

Q1 What do you usually do on layovers?

Q2 What is the nicest airport that you have ever had a layover in? What did you do there?

5. Situational Collocations

Complete the sentences using the collocations from the word box.

Word Box

- make my transfer
- ticket holders
- gate check
- traveling solo
- file a claim
- head to the gate
- boarding time
- begin boarding

1. This lounge is for business class _____ only.
2. The flight attendant asked me to _____ my bag because of its size.
3. I'm not sure if I'm going to be able to _____.
4. We still have an hour until _____. Do you want to get a drink?
5. Under which circumstances am I eligible to _____ for delayed flight compensation?
6. I usually prefer _____, so I don't have to worry about pleasing other people.
7. I think it's time for us to _____.
8. The flight is scheduled to _____ soon.

6. What Would You Do?

Read the situation and explain what you would do in that situation.

Extended Layover

Flight delays could happen for any number of reasons, including medical emergencies, mechanical problems with the airline, difficult weather conditions, or security issues related to the aircraft. Your flight was just delayed because of one of these issues, which means that you will miss your connecting flight to your final destination. You will not arrive until tomorrow morning, so you will need to book a hotel in the area and delay the rest of your travel places. You are also concerned that your baggage might not make it to its final destination.

Q1. Who would you ask at the airport to help your problem? What would you say?

Q2. Are there any other things that you would need to contact people outside of the airport to reschedule?

Q3. Do you think the airline should compensate you for your troubles?

How Much Do I Pay?

Some airlines have begun charging additional fees to occupy premium seats, including coveted window and aisle seats. This, of course, makes it more difficult for families traveling on the same plane to sit in adjacent seats without paying an additional fee to occupy the window and aisle seats in one row. By choosing to not pay the premium, they are stuck sitting in center seats in different rows. One journal magazine had an interesting story explaining airline expenses and profits. Not surprisingly, flying is not a very profitable business, at least not for most airlines. The profit earned from ticket revenue (return on sales), including taxes, is less than 1%. As the graphic on the right shows, the prices paid by 99 out of 100 passengers go to cover the airline's costs.

Q. Do you have any tips for getting a good deal on a flight?

Decoding a Flight

In a hypothetical flight with 100 passengers, it takes fares and fees from 99 seats to cover all costs.

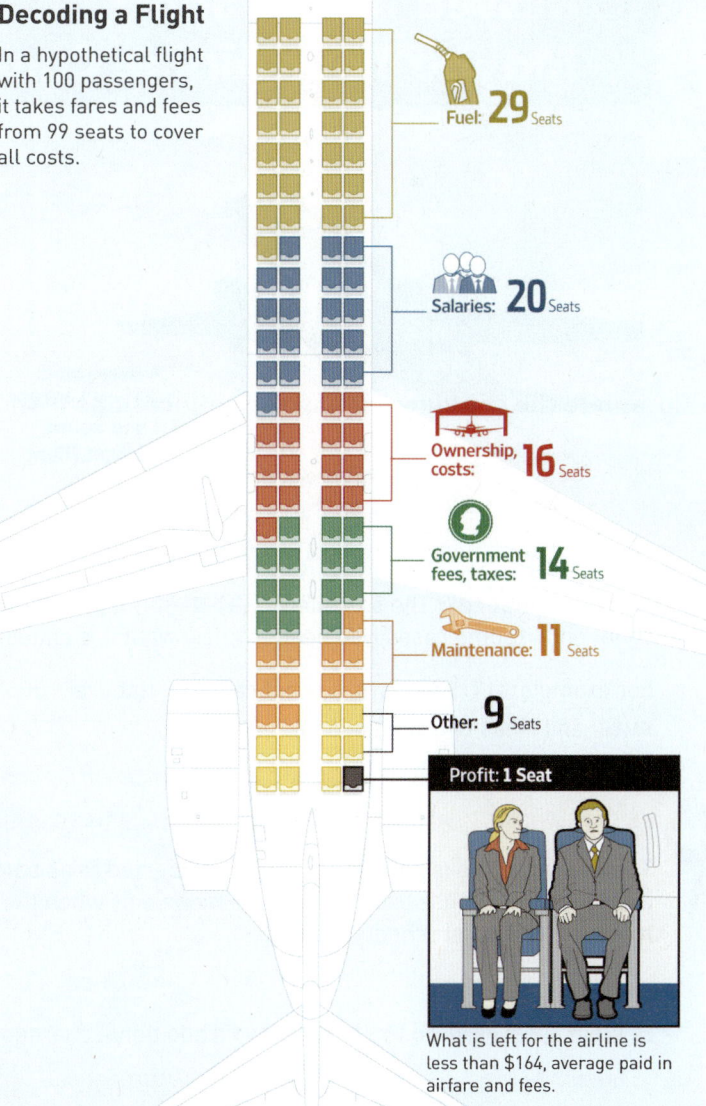

Fuel: 29 Seats
Salaries: 20 Seats
Ownership costs: 16 Seats
Government fees, taxes: 14 Seats
Maintenance: 11 Seats
Other: 9 Seats
Profit: 1 Seat

What is left for the airline is less than $164, average paid in airfare and fees.

7. Cultural Discussion Questions

Read the passage and talk about the questions in as much detail as possible.

Catch Your Flight

It can be very frustrating to miss a scheduled flight, whether it is your fault or not. Here are some tips to help you ensure that you make it smoothly to your final destination. First, when booking a flight with a connection, make sure that there is enough time between transfers that, even if there is a slight delay, you will still be able to make your connection. Second, arrive at the airport at least two hours before your scheduled departure time. Finally, prepare for the security check while you are still waiting in line for the scanners. Remove all metal items from your pockets and also jackets, hats, and footwear if requested. By doing these things, you have a greater chance of making it to the gate in time.

1. What is the best strategy to ensure that you will not miss your flight?
2. What should you do if you miss your flight, even when following these strategies?

Missed Your Flight? Maybe Your Airline Can Help.

Wait for me! I haven't boarded yet!

Never mind. Just pay RM100 and board the next flight

If you are delayed on your way to the airport because of a summer thunderstorm, you might think you are out of luck. Most airlines now gladly charge you a full walk-up fare for the next flight.

Here is a secret: The so-called **"flat tire" rule** still exists. You just have to remind the ticket agent and in some cases, you need to know what it is called.

For example, at US Airways, it is not called a "flat tire" rule. It is referred to as the **"two-hour" rule,** and it has two stipulations:

① The passenger arrives at the airport no later than two hours after the departure of their flight.
② The passenger must standby on flights from the same airline as their ticketed flight.

The two-hour rule is not to be solicited or referred to as part of fare rules to circumvent voluntary changes. An in-house exception can be made only when the passenger has made an attempt to make the originally scheduled flight.

Q. What other ways do you know to avoid additional charges for a missed flight?

Lesson 10 / Travel Delays **69**

8. If You Ask Me

Read the discussion topic and select the statement that you believe in the most. Then role-play the scenario.

The Rising Cost of Air Travel

Air travel is becoming more and more expensive these days. Airlines are now charging for meals, snacks, entertainment, and even the seat that you choose for the flight. Meanwhile, the seats seem to be getting smaller, and the previous two-bag rule has been dropped to only one bag, with an extra fee for extra baggage. Airlines say this is because of the rising cost of fuel and running the airline.

Topic Question

Do you think airlines should be able to charge for these extra services (supportive), or should they be complementary for the passenger (non-supportive)?

Supportive Opinion VS **Non-Supportive Opinion**

Role-play

Act out the role-play using the slang and idioms and useful expressions.

Situation

You just barely missed your flight because of unusually bad traffic on the way to the airport. You need to get on a flight tonight because of an important meeting at your destination. You are at the airline check-in desk now requesting a boarding pass for the next flight. Politely tell the worker about your problem and try to convince him or her to help you with no additional fees.

Role A
- Explain why you are late for the flight.
- Politely ask if he or she is able to help you.

Role B
- Sympathize with the passenger about the situation.
- Offer a ticket on the next flight departing in two hours.

Wrapping Up! Tell four things that you learned from this lesson and review.

1 2 3 4

11 International Conflicts

Learning Objective
Upon completion of this lesson you will be able to **discuss international diplomacy.**

Expression Check
- ☑ These two countries have been at odds for as long as I can remember.
- ☑ This is a perfect example of what conflict can do.
- ☑ One of these countries needs to extend the olive branch.

1. Warm Up Activity
Talk about the questions.

1. What international conflicts have you seen in the news recently?
2. Is serving in the military compulsory in your country?
3. How would you feel if your country went to war with another country?

2. Useful Phrases
Match the phrases (a-d) to the phrases (1-4) to form a complete sentence. The useful phrases are italicized.

A *This is a perfect example of*

B Why can't everyone

C Those two countries *have been at odds with* each other

D One of these countries needs to

1 *for as long as I can remember.*

2 *extend an olive branch.*

3 what conflict can do.

4 *just get along?*

3. Slang & Idioms

Check out the slang and idioms and try to make your own sentences.

A	**settle a score** : to retaliate or get revenge for a previous wrong	*Philip insists he's not interested in settling a score against the man that fired him.*
B	**bone of contention** : an issue that is causing a long-standing disagreement	*Jerry leaving his dirty dishes in the sink became a bone of contention between him and his roommate.*
C	**ceasefire** : a temporary end to hostilities	*The latest ceasefire seems to be holding.*
D	**extend an olive branch** : do something in order to show that you want to stop arguing	*The government is extending an olive branch to the demonstrators.*

4. Key Conversation

Read through the dialogue and practice with a partner.

A Score to Settle

David Hey! Did you watch the news last night?

Samir You mean about that couple that was kidnapped from that resort?

David Yeah, it was kind of hard to miss. They must have had it on every channel.

Samir Yeah, they said extremists did it. This is the third kidnapping this month. The Americans don't seem too pleased at this news.

David No doubt! It's the American tourists they've been targeting. If you ask me, they should just go in there with the army and settle the score once and for all.

Samir I don't know. I don't think any of this violence will really solve anything. I mean, can't everyone just get along?

David Would you say that if it were your family that they took? These guys know they can get away with it. That's why this is happening so much.

Samir Still. You've seen what violence does. They'll probably call themselves martyrs for the cause or something.

David So you would rather just pay them the ransom money?

Samir No, but there has to be a better solution out there.

Questions
1. Why do you think the tourists were captured?
2. Do you think that David is right that violence is necessary for a situation like this?

International Conflicts

What's Your Personality Type?

The concept of a behavior profile was developed in the late 1920s as a result of psychologist Dr. William Marston's theory that there are four basic personality types - **D for Dominant, I for Influencer, S for Steady, and C for Compliant** (or DISC for short).

Over the years, different versions of the same theory developed including BEST (Bold-Expressive-Sympathetic-Technical) and Dr. Gary Couture's version using bird names (Dove, Owl, Peacock, and Eagle).

We fit into one of these basic personality types, which define the way we interact with other people, the way we go about life, our motivations, and how we succeed.

They are:

Dove: The dove is people-orientated, loyal, friendly, hard-working, and a great team player but tends to avoid change, confrontation, risk-taking, and assertiveness.

Owl: The owl is logical, mathematically minded, methodical, and sometimes seen as a perfectionist. The owl can be slow to make decisions and inflexible if rules and logic say otherwise. Owls are not big risk-takers, but love detail.

Peacock: The peacock loves talking, loves to be the center of attention, has passion/enthusiasm, and is happy/optimistic. Peacocks can be accused of talking too much, and they are not good with detail or time-control.

Eagle: Eagles are dominant, stimulated by challenge, decisive, and direct. Eagles can be blunt/stubborn, can lose sight of the big picture, and can be insensitive to other people's needs. They are natural achievers.

Q1. Which bird do you think best describes your personality type?

Q2. Which other kinds of personalities do you like to surround yourself with?

5. Situational Collocations

Complete the sentences using the collocations from the word box.

Word Box

- uneasy peace
- pick a fight
- collateral damage
- deliberate on the issue
- hinders progress
- destabilizing conflict
- international tensions
- diplomatic pressure

1. Representatives from both countries gathered to _____.
2. The incident has once again stirred up _____.
3. The policy targets anyone who entered the country illegally, so refugees have become _____.
4. An _____ followed in the first days of the ceasefire.
5. Wealth inequality threatens democracy by creating _____.
6. For months they have been applying intense economic and _____.
7. I feel like they are desperate to _____ with us.
8. His poor attitude _____ in the negotiations.

Lesson 11 / International Conflicts   73

6. What Would You Do?

Read the situation and explain what you would do in that situation.

Working with the Enemy

Recently, refugees from a war-torn country have been entering your country in great numbers. Many local people worry about the dangers that the influx of new residents may pose to the local economy. Furthermore, you have heard rumors that some of them entering illegally could be dangerous criminals. You aren't sure what to believe. You just learned that a refugee family is moving into your building. Your roommate wants to go and welcome them and offer to help them settle into the neighborhood.

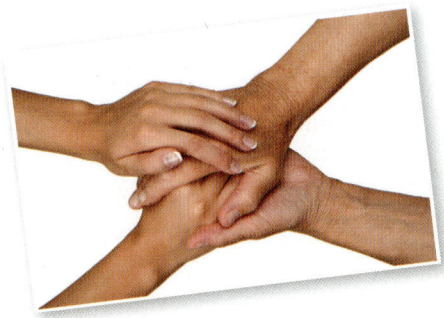

Q1. What would you do in that situation?

Q2. What might the family need help with?

Q3. In your opinion, is it dangerous to stereotype people from different groups?

Do We Live in Peace?

Peace and sustainability are the cornerstones of humanity in the 21st century. The major challenges facing humanity today are global climate change, accessible fresh water, ever decreasing bio-diversity, wars, and over population. Not only are our natural resources at risk, but human conflicts over religion and politics are increasing.

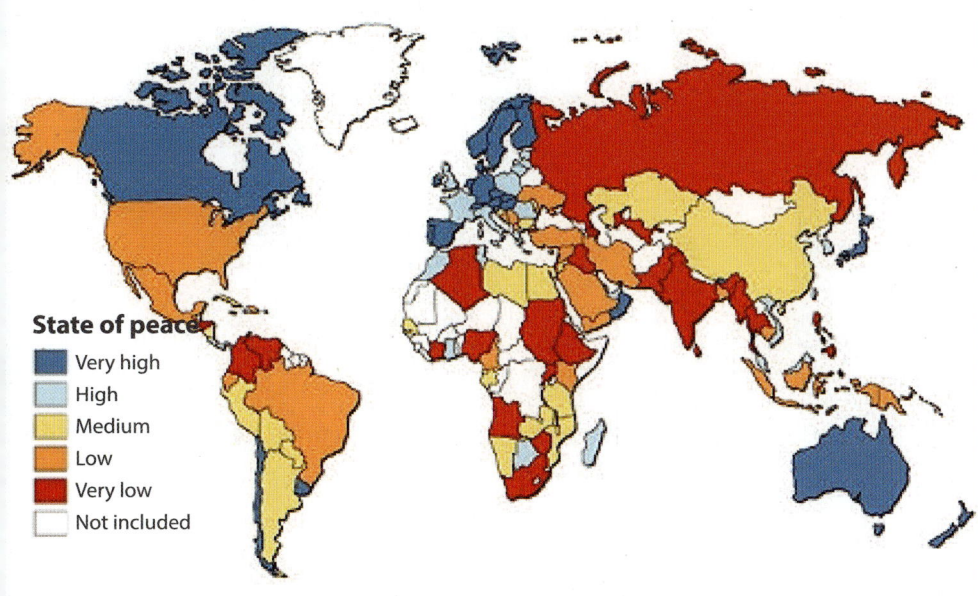

State of peace
- Very high
- High
- Medium
- Low
- Very low
- Not included

Q1 Do you think your government is doing enough? What would you like to see happen?

Q2 How can we as individuals encourage the government to seek peaceful solutions to international conflicts?

Q3 Do you feel that it is your country's duty to help less fortunate people around the world?

Q4 How can we better preserve the Earth's resources for future generations?

International Conflicts

7. Cultural Discussion Questions

Read the passage and talk about the questions in as much detail as possible.

World at War

With the advent of modern military technology, the last 150 years have been described as the bloodiest in human history, with over 108 million people being killed in armed conflict in the 20th century alone. During a war, even those who remain back at home struggle, as prices for necessities increase due to production slowing down. Despite the efforts of organizations committed to promoting peace, many countries still turn to violence as a solution to their problems.

1. Do you think world peace will ever be possible? Why or why not?
2. How has your country been affected by war in recent years?

The State of the World Isn't So Bad

According to a new report from the Human Security Report Project, the number of deaths from armed conflicts around the world continues to fall, even while inter-communal wars have jumped and other conflicts have become increasingly difficult to bring to an end.

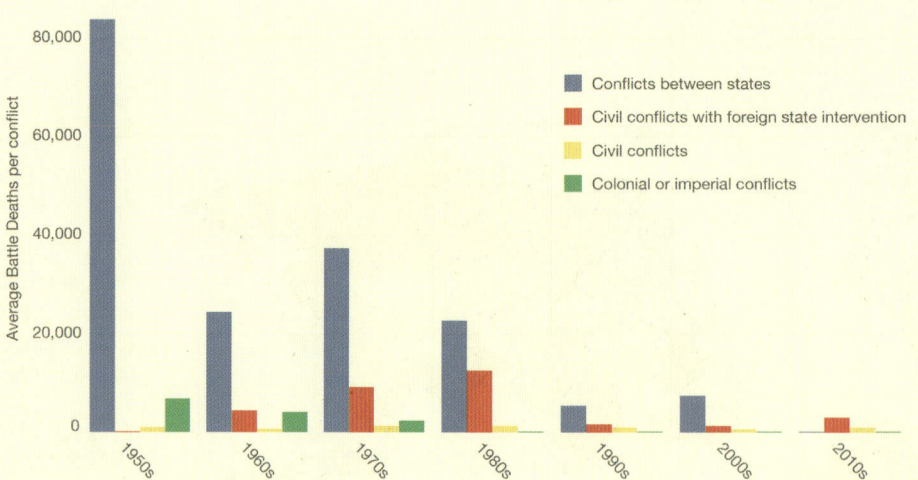

Average Number of Battle Deaths Per Conflict Since 1946, By Type

There has been a steady decline in the number of international conflicts—defined here to include interstate and extrastate conflicts—around the world.

Q1. Do you think that the data shows a positive trend?
Q2. Do you expect the number of armed conflicts to continue to fall in the coming decades? Why or why not?

Lesson 11 / International Conflicts

8. If You Ask Me

Read the discussion topic and select the statement that you believe in the most. Then role-play the scenario.

Dodging the Draft

Because war requires a large number of active soldiers, some countries find it necessary to require citizens to serve in the military if they do not receive a sufficient number of volunteers. Compulsory military service, or the draft, is sometimes controversial as it requires young people to sacrifice their personal goals and beliefs to join in the fighting. In times of war, some young people have resorted to illegal tactics, such as faking an injury or moving to another country, to dodge the draft. Each person has their own reasons for not wanting to serve in the military, but it is often because they dislike the idea of killing others for a cause they do not agree with.

Supportive Opinion

VS

Non-Supportive Opinion

Topic Question

Should the government be allowed to draft soldiers, or should individuals have the right to choose whether or not to serve?

Role-play

Act out the role-play using the slang and idioms and useful expressions.

Situation

You and a co-worker are watching the news on TV at a bar after work. The current story involves another eruption of violence between two countries that have been at war for as long as you can remember. You are not even sure what originally started the conflict, but the losses on both sides have been enormous. You strongly feel that one of the countries should just give up and extend an olive branch. Ask your co-worker for his or her opinion on the situation and whether he or she believes that world peace will ever be possible.

Role A
- Tell your co-worker what you think of the situation.
- Ask for his or her opinion.

Role B
- Agree that the war seems pointless.
- Share your opinion on world peace with your partner.

Wrapping Up!

Tell four things that you learned from this lesson and review.

| 1 | 2 | 3 | 4 |

12 I Wish I'd Done Something Differently

Learning Objective

Upon completion of this lesson you will be able to **express regret for things you have or haven't done.**

Expression Check

- ☑ I'm never doing that again as long as I live.
- ☑ I totally regret taking my parents' advice.
- ☑ I wish I would've just followed my heart.

1. Warm Up Activity

Talk about the questions.

1. What is something that you regretted after doing?
2. Is there anything that you really wish you had done that you didn't?
3. Have you ever taken someone's advice and regretted it later?

2. Useful Phrases

Match the phrases (a-d) to the phrases (1-4) to form a complete sentence. The useful phrases are italicized.

A. I'm never *doing that again*
B. I *totally regret*
C. I *wish I would've just*
D. I've *replayed the events*

1. taking my parents' advice.
2. again and again in my head.
3. followed my heart.
4. as long as I live.

3. Slang & Idioms

Check out the slang and idioms and try to make your own sentences.

A	**a falling out** : a quarrel or disagreement	Nadine had a falling out with her sister over a family inheritance.
B	**a do-over** : a new opportunity to do something after a previous attempt has been unsuccessful	I'd love to have a do-over of my time in college.
C	**that ship has sailed** : the opportunity has passed	There's no point in calling him back. That ship has sailed.
D	**be kicking oneself for doing something** : to blame or criticize oneself for something one has done	I'm kicking myself for not taking that job.

4. Key Conversation

Read through the dialogue and practice with a partner.

I've Replayed It Again and Again

Melinda	Patrick, have you ever just wished you could have a do-over in life? I completely botched things up with the boss, and I'm afraid I've lost my chance for a promotion.
Patrick	Everybody wants a reset button, for sure. What happened?
Melinda	I misplaced the files for the big case I'd been researching for months, and he went ballistic. I've replayed what happened again and again in my head, and I just can't understand how I screwed up so royally.
Patrick	I'm sorry you're having such a tough time. I'm sure Marty will get over it in time. Hey, can I lend a hand?
Melinda	I just keep kicking myself for not thinking ahead. If only I'd made backup copies, this never would have happened, and I'd be sipping cocktails with the girls right now instead of rewriting everything. Nah, thanks, but you should go ahead home.
Patrick	Well, you have my cell if you need someone in your corner.

Questions

1. Do you think Melinda really lost her shot at a promotion?
2. What do you think Melinda could have done differently?

I Wish I'd Done Something Differently

9 Things No One Wants to Regret When They Are Older

Every one of us has experienced feelings of regret, but it is not too late to set things straight. We are still here breathing. Right now, we have an opportunity to change our futures. Right now, we can choose to erase regret from our later years.

Here are nine things no one wants to regret when they are older.

1. Not spending enough time smiling with the people you love.
2. Holding a grudge and never forgiving someone you care about.
3. Fulfilling everyone else's dreams instead of your own.
4. Not being honest about how you feel.
5. Being foolish and irresponsible with your finances.
6. Getting caught up in needless drama and negativity.
7. Never making your own happiness a priority.
8. Never making a difference in the lives of others.
9. Failing because you were scared to fail.

"A decision is your choice. Once you have decided, stick with it. You will never regret it."

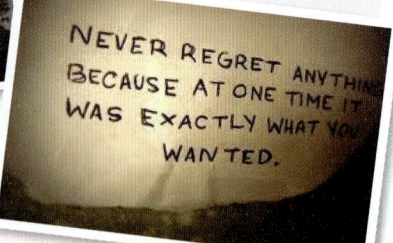

Q1. What is a lesson you have learned from your regrets?

Q2. What can you do to avoid having regrets and live your life to the fullest?

5. Situational Collocations

Complete the sentences using the collocations from the word box.

Word Box

- a second chance
- showed some hesitation
- feels absolutely sick about
- filled with sorrow
- haunting memory
- doomed to failure
- fixating on the past
- think over

1. Please _____ what you've just said, and get back to me.
2. Her eyes were _____ as she told the story.
3. If I had _____, I'd do things differently.
4. You don't want to waste your life _____.
5. Travis _____ to do her a favor.
6. He _____ what happened.
7. That day is still a _____ for me.
8. If you keep on ignoring my advice, your plan will be _____.

6. What Would You Do?

Read the situation and explain what you would do in that situation.

Unspoken Feelings

You are online, cruising through pages on the latest SNS, when you come across a face you have not seen in a long time. The person you see was an old best friend from high school who you were secretly in love with. You were always too shy to express your feelings, and you have always wondered what would have happened if you had been more courageous. You have not spoken to the person in about 10 years, but you see that he/she is still single. A friend wants to talk with you about why you look so absorbed in thought right now.

Q1. What would you tell your friend about the situation?

Q2. Do you think you should contact that person?

Q3. Do you have any regrets from when you were in high school?

Past, Present, and Future

How much time do you spend constantly switching between worrying about the future and regretting the past or experiencing and feeling the wonders that are happening in the present moment?

If you are self-aware enough to realize that your thinking state is dominated by circular rumination over what has happened in the past, what techniques or practices could you employ to redirect more of your thinking time to the present moment? Can one actually "control" his/her thinking state? Is there any way to redirect your thoughts in a more productive way?

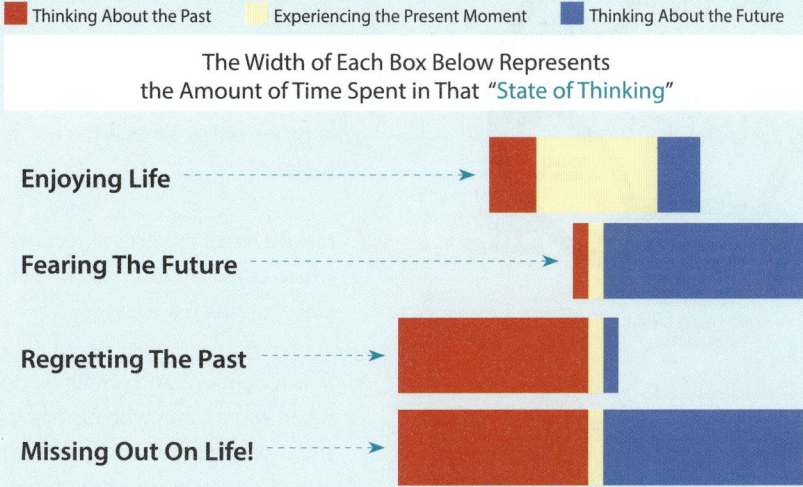

Q1. What are some things you think you missed out on in life?

Q2. What do you enjoy most about your life?

7. Cultural Discussion Questions

Read the passage and talk about the questions in as much detail as possible.

Decision-Making in the Family

In some cultures, young people view the opinions of elders as more important than their own desires when making important decisions. They choose to defer decision-making responsibilities to the older generation instead of following their own hearts and sometimes come to regret it later. Important life decisions, including one's career path and spouse, may be decided by someone who isn't directly involved.

1. Do you think it is wise to follow the advice of your parents or older members of your community?
2. What are the possible repercussions of dismissing or following your elders' advice?

Make a Good Decision – Then You Won't Have Any Regrets

Why do we sometimes regret the choices we make? The obvious answer is that we sometimes make bad choices, with unforeseen negative consequences. But that is not the only time we experience the pain of regret. In fact, we routinely regret perfectly good choices – not because of the outcome, but because of our *experience choosing*.

The Keys to Making a Good Decision

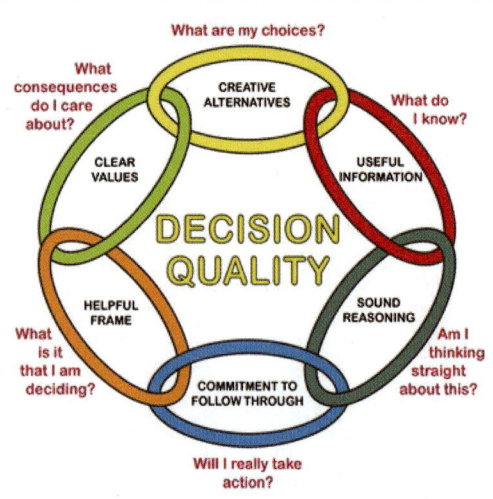

1. Identify the decision to be made as well as the objectives or outcome you want to achieve.

2. Brainstorm and come up with several possible choices.

3. Weigh the probabilities or possible outcomes. In other words, what is the worst that can happen?

4. Make a list of the pros and cons. Prioritize which considerations are very important to you and which are less so.

5. Solicit opinions and obtain feedback from those you trust or who have had a similar situation to contend with. There may be some aspects you have not thought about.

6. Make the decision and monitor your results.

Q1 What is the best/worst decision you have ever made?

Q2 How do you usually deliberate important decisions?

Lesson 12 / I Wish I'd Done Something Differently

8. If You Ask Me

Read the discussion topic and select the statement that you believe in the most. Then role-play the scenario.

A Less Painful Regret?

People's opinions vary tremendously on whether it is better to regret something you have or have not done. When making a difficult decision, some (supportive) people say that it is best to just go for it and try even though it may turn out to be a huge, painful mistake. (non-supportive) Others say that it is better to risk the regret of passing by an opportunity or choosing not to pursue something because it may keep them from being hurt or experiencing failure.

Topic Question

Do you prefer to take chances regardless of the risks or would you rather play it safe and choose the easier path?

Supportive Opinion

VS

Non-Supportive Opinion

Role-play

Act out the role-play using the slang and idioms and useful expressions.

Situation

You are currently employed at an international company. You were recently offered a transfer to an overseas branch. Unsure what to do, you asked your parents for advice and they told you that you would be lonely and would regret taking the job, so you turned the opportunity down. Since then, you have come to deeply regret your decision. One of your co-workers accepted the job and seems to be having the time of her life. Every time you see her social media posts about her exciting life abroad, you are filled with regret. Tell one of your friends about your problem.

Role A
- Explain the situation to your friend.
- Tell about how you feel.

Role B
- Advise your friend that it is unwise to live in the past.
- Suggest he or she apply for a similar position the next time one is available.

Wrapping Up!

Tell four things that you learned from this lesson and review.

1.   2.   3.   4.

New Get Up To Speed+ Book 6
SLANG & IDIOM GLOSSARY

Lesson 1

catch some Z's	to get some sleep
catnap	a short, light sleep; a doze
shuteye	sleep
snooze	to sleep for a short period

Lesson 2

block party	a party for all the residents of a block or neighborhood
fair-weather friend	a person who stops being a friend in times of difficulty
next-door neighbor	a person living in the house or apartment closest to one's own
tightly-knit	united or bound together by strong relationships and common interests

Lesson 3

as different as night and day	as different as possible
closed-minded	unreceptive to new ideas or arguments
set aside one's differences	to forget about or set aside the things that one disagrees with
sheltered	protected from difficulties or unpleasant realities

Lesson 4

cry over spilled milk	to express regret about something that has already happened or cannot be changed
kick oneself	to blame or criticize oneself for something one has done
latchkey kid	a child who is at home without adult supervision for some part of the day
live in the past	to always be thinking about things that have already happened

Lesson 5

diplomatic immunity	the privilege of exemption from certain laws and taxes granted to diplomats working abroad
free trade	international trade left to its natural course without tariffs or other restrictions
hostility	acts of warfare or other negative diplomatic behavior
strike an accord	to make an agreement

Lesson 6

a storm brewing	extreme weather is coming
blow over	go away without serious consequences
flood out	have to leave one's home because of a flood
twister	a tornado

Lesson 7

breaking news	newly received information about an event that is currently occurring
fresh off the wire	newly released news; usually sensational and exciting
off the record	not made as an official or attributable statement
scoop	a piece of news published by a newspaper or broadcast by a television station before its rivals

Lesson 8

a new lease on life	a substantially improved chance at leading a happy or successful life
out with the old, in with the new	to leave old things or ideas behind and start fresh with new ones
turn the page	make a fresh start
with a clean slate	start again with a fresh beginning, unencumbered by regrets from the past

Lesson 9

anti-piracy laws	laws aimed at reducing the illegal download of media
elevator music	boring background music for stores and other public places
file sharing	using a computer network to provide information to others
strike a chord	affect or stir someone's emotions

Lesson 10

bumped up / down	be changed from the seat you paid for to another class
jetlag	extreme tiredness felt by a person after a long flight across several time zones
layover	a period of rest or waiting before the next stage in a journey
red-eye	an overnight flight

Lesson 11

bone of contention	an issue that is causing a long-standing disagreement
ceasefire	a temporary end to hostilities
extend an olive branch	do something in order to show that you want to stop arguing
settle a score	to retaliate or get revenge for a previous wrong

Lesson 12

a do-over	a new opportunity to do something after a previous attempt has been unsuccessful
a falling out	a quarrel or disagreement
be kicking oneself for doing something	to blame or criticize oneself for something one has done
that ship has sailed	the opportunity has passed

New Get Up To Speed+ Book 6
ANSWER KEY

Lesson 1

Useful Phrases

a 1
b 4
c 3
d 2

Situational Collocations

1 fast asleep
2 bedtime routine
3 Sleep deprivation
4 utterly exhausted
5 light doze
6 deep sleeper
7 restless night
8 wide awake

Lesson 2

Useful Phrases

a 3
b 1
c 4
d 2

Situational Collocations

1 closely related
2 friendly approach
3 warm smile
4 welcoming committee
5 considerable hospitality
6 lifelong friendship
7 get together
8 drop by

Lesson 3

Useful Phrases

a 3
b 1
c 2
d 4

Situational Collocations

1 intercultural communication
2 diverse viewpoints
3 mainstream acceptance
4 fundamental differences
5 social setting
6 direct manner
7 show respect
8 starting point

Lesson 4

Useful Phrases

a 4
b 2
c 1
d 3

Situational Collocations

1 spending quality time
2 take a day
3 deeply regretted
4 seized an opportunity
5 work-life balance
6 juggling responsibilities
7 regrets bitterly
8 opportunity cost

Lesson 5

Useful Phrases

a 3
b 1
c 4
d 2

Situational Collocations

1. sever ties
2. through diplomatic channels
3. negotiate peace
4. reach an agreement
5. share credit
6. significant misunderstanding
7. situation unfolds
8. settle the dispute

Lesson 6

Useful Phrases

a 3
b 1
c 4
d 2

Situational Collocations

1. emergency preparedness
2. seek shelter
3. storm clouds
4. automated alert
5. heavy rain
6. emergency exit
7. disaster relief
8. inclement weather

Lesson 7

Useful Phrases

a 4
b 3
c 1
d 2

Situational Collocations

1. declining circulation
2. gauge the reaction
3. broadcast journalism
4. gain publicity
5. heavily debated
6. eyewitness reports
7. make the news
8. disseminate fake news

Lesson 8

Useful Phrases

a 3
b 4
c 2
d 1

Situational Collocations

1. minimize the damage
2. start over
3. inevitable conclusion
4. bound to end up
5. lingering concerns
6. step forward
7. dwell on this problem
8. reassess your decision

Lesson 9

Useful Phrases

a 4
b 1
c 2
d 3

Situational Collocations

1. time-consuming process
2. violating the law
3. hack into
4. launched its service
5. streaming a video
6. victimless crime

New Get Up To Speed+ Book 6
ANSWER KEY

7 click a link
8 available for download

Lesson 10

Useful Phrases

a 4
b 2
c 1
d 3

Situational Collocations

1 ticket holders
2 gate check
3 make my transfer
4 boarding time
5 file a claim
6 traveling solo
7 head to the gate
8 begin boarding

Lesson 11

Useful Phrases

a 3
b 4
c 1
d 2

Situational Collocations

1 deliberate on the issue
2 international tensions
3 collateral damage
4 uneasy peace
5 destabilizing conflict
6 diplomatic pressure
7 pick a fight
8 hinders progress

Lesson 12

Useful Phrases

a 4
b 1
c 3
d 2

Situational Collocations

1 think over
2 filled with sorrow
3 a second chance
4 fixating on the past
5 showed some hesitation
6 feels absolutely sick about
7 haunting memory
8 doomed to failure